WALL STREET
AND THE RISE OF HITLER

WALL STREET
AND THE RISE OF HITLER

ANTONY C. SUTTON

Seal Beach, California

Published by:

'76 Press
P.O. Box 2686
Seal Beach, Calif. 90740

Library of Congress Catalog Card Number 76-14011
International Standard Book Number 0-89245-004-5

MANUFACTURED IN THE UNITED STATES OF AMERICA

Dedication

Dedicated to the memory of Floyd Paxton —
entrepreneur, inventor, writer, and American, who
believed in and worked for individual rights in a
free society under the Constitution.

CONTENTS

PART TWO: Wall Street and Funds for Hitler

PREFACE

This is the third and final volume of a trilogy describing the role of the American corporate socialists, otherwise known as the Wall Street financial elite or the Eastern Liberal Establishment, in three significant twentieth-century historical events: the 1917 Lenin-Trotsky Revolution in Russia, the 1933 election of Franklin D. Roosevelt in the United States, and the 1933 seizure of power by Adolf Hitler in Germany.

Each of these events introduced some variant of socialism into a major country — *i.e.*, Bolshevik socialism in Russia, New Deal socialism in the United States, and National socialism in Germany.

Contemporary academic histories, with perhaps the sole exception of Carroll Quigley's *Tragedy And Hope*, ignore this evidence. On the other hand, it is understandable that universities and research organizations, dependent on financial aid from foundations that are controlled by this same New York financial elite, would hardly want to support and to publish research on these aspects of international politics. The bravest of trustees is unlikely to bite the hand that feeds his organization.

It is also eminently clear from the evidence in this trilogy that "public-spirited businessmen" do not journey to Washington as lobbyists and administrators in order to serve the United States. They are in Washington to serve their own profit-maximizing interests. Their purpose is not to further a competitive, free-market economy, but to manipulate a politicized regime, call it what you will, to their own advantage.

It is business manipulation of Hitler's accession to power in March 1933 that is the topic of *Wall Street and the Rise of Hitler*.

ANTONY C. SUTTON

July, 1976

INTRODUCTION
Unexplored Facets of Naziism

Since the early 1920s unsubstantiated reports have circulated to the effect that not only German industrialists, but also Wall Street financiers, had some role — possibly a substantial role — in the rise of Hitler and Naziism. This book presents previously unpublished evidence, a great deal from files of the Nuremburg Military Tribunals, to support this hypothesis. However, the full impact and suggestiveness of the evidence cannot be found from reading this volume alone. Two previous books in this series, *Wall Street and the Bolshevik Revolution*[1] and *Wall Street and FDR*,[2] described the roles of the same firms, and often the same individuals and their fellow directors, hard at work manipulating and assisting the Bolshevik revolution in Russia in 1917, backing Franklin D. Roosevelt for President in the United States in 1933, as well as aiding the rise of Hitler in pre-war Germany. In brief, this book is part of a more extensive study of the rise of modern socialism and the corporate socialists.

This politically active Wall Street group is more or less the same elitist circle known generally among Conservatives as the "Liberal Establishment," by liberals (for instance G. William Domhoff) as "the ruling class,"[3] and by conspiratorial theorists Gary Allen[4] and Dan Smoot[5] as the "Insiders." But whatever we call this self-perpetuating elitist group, it is apparently fundamentally significant in the determination of world affairs, at a level far behind and above that of the elected politicians.

The influence and work of this same group in the rise of Hitler and Nazi Germany is the topic of this book. This is an area of historical research almost totally unexplored by the academic world. It is an historical minefield for the unwary and the careless not aware of the intricacies of research procedures. The Soviets have long accused Wall Street bankers of backing international fascism, but their own record of historical accuracy hardly lends their accusations much credence in the West, and they do not of course criticize support of their own brand of fascism.

This author falls into a different camp. Previously accused of being overly critical of Sovietism and domestic socialism, while ignoring Wall Street and the rise of Hitler, this book hopefully will redress an assumed and quite inaccurate philosophical imbalance and emphasize the real point at issue: Whatever you call the collectivist system — Soviet socialism, New Deal socialism, corporate socialism, or National socialism — it is the average citizen, the guy in the street, that ultimately loses out to the boys running the operation at the top. Each system in its own way is a system of plunder, an organizational device to get everyone living (or attempting to live) at the expense of everyone else, while the elitist leaders, the rulers and the politicians, scalp the cream off the top.

The role of this American power elite in the rise of Hitler should also be viewed in conjunction with a little-known aspect of Hitlerism only now being explored: the mystical origins of Naziism, and its relations with the Thule Society and with other conspiratorial groups. This author is no expert on occultism or conspiracy, but it is obvious that the mystical origins, the neo-pagan historical roots of Naziism, the Bavarian Illuminati and the Thule Society, are relatively unknown areas yet to be explored by technically competent researchers. Some research is already recorded in French; probably the best introduction in English is a translation of *Hitler et la Tradition Cathare* by Jean Michel Angebert.[6]

Angebert reveals the 1933 crusade of *Schutzstaffel* member Otto Rahn in search of the Holy Grail, which was supposedly located in the Cathar stronghold in Southern France. The early Nazi hierarchy (Hitler and Himmler, as well as Rudolph Hess and Rosenberg) was steeped in a neo-pagan theology, in part associated with the Thule Society, whose ideals were close to those of the Bavarian Illuminati. This was a submerged driving force behind Naziism, with a powerful mystical hold over the hard-core S.S. faithful. Our contemporary establishment historians barely mention, let alone explore, these occult origins; consequently, they miss an element equally as important as the financial origins of National Socialism.

In 1950 James Stewart Martin published a very readable book, *All Honorable Men*,[7] describing his experiences as Chief of the Economic Warfare Section of the Department of Justice investigating the structure of Nazi industry. Martin asserts that American and British businessmen got themselves appointed to key positions in this post-war investigation to divert, stifle and muffle investigation of Nazi industrialists and so keep hidden their own involvement. One British officer was sentenced by court martial to two years in jail for protecting a Nazi, and several American officials were removed from their positions. Why would American and British businessmen want to protect Nazi businessmen? In public they argued that these were merely German businessmen who had nothing to do with the Nazi regime and were innocent of complicity in Nazi conspiracies. Martin does not explore this explanation in depth, but he is obviously unhappy and skeptical about it. The evidence suggests there was a concerted effort not only to protect Nazi businessmen, but also to protect the collaborating elements from American and British business.

The German businessmen could have disclosed a lot of uncomfortable facts. In return for protection, they told very little. It is undoubtedly *not* coincidental that the Hitler industrialists on trial at Nuremburg received less than a slap on the wrist. We raise the question of whether the Nuremburg trials should not have been held in Washington — with a few prominent U.S. businessmen as well as Nazi businessmen in the dock!

Two extracts from contemporary sources will introduce and suggest the theme to be expanded. The first extract is from Roosevelt's own files. The U.S. Ambassador in Germany, William Dodd, wrote FDR from Berlin on October 19, 1936 (three years after Hitler came to power), concerning American industrialists and their aid to the Nazis:

> *Much as I believe in peace as our best policy, I cannot avoid the fears which Wilson emphasized more than once in conversations with me, August 15, 1915 and later: the breakdown of democracy in all Europe will be a disaster to the people. But what can you do? At the present moment more than a hundred American corporations have subsidiaries here or cooperative understandings. The DuPonts have three allies in Germany that are aiding in the armament business. Their chief ally is the I. G. Farben Company, a part of the Government which gives 200,000 marks a year to one propaganda organization operating on American opinion. Standard Oil Company (New York subcompany) sent $2,000,000 here in December 1933 and has made $500,000 a year helping Germans make Ersatz gas for war purposes; but Standard Oil cannot take any of its earnings out of the country except in goods. They do little of this, report their earnings at home, but do not explain the facts. The International Harvester Company president told me their business here rose 33% a year (arms manufacture, I believe), but they could take nothing out. Even our airplanes people have secret arrangement*

with Krupps. General Motor Company and Ford do enormous businesses [sic] here through their subsidiaries and take no profits out. I mention these facts because they complicate things and add to war dangers.[8]

Second, a quote from the diary of the same U.S. Ambassador in Germany. The reader should bear in mind that a representative of the cited Vacuum Oil Company — as well as representatives of other Nazi-supporting American firms — was appointed to the post-war Control Commission to de-Nazify the Nazis:

> *January 23. Thursday. Our Commercial Attache brought Dr. Engelbrecht, chairman of the Vacuum Oil Company in Hamburg, to see me. Engelbrecht repeated what he had said a year ago: "The Standard Oil Company of New York, the parent company of the Vacuum, has spent 10,000,000 marks in Germany trying to find oil resources and building a great refinery near the Hamburg harbor." Engelbrecht is still boring wells and finding a good deal of crude oil in the Hanover region, but he had no hope of great deposits. He hopes Dr. Schacht will subsidize his company as he does some German companies that have found no crude oil. The Vacuum spends all its earnings here, employs 1,000 men and never sends any of its money home. I could give him no encouragement . . . .*[9]

And further:

> *These men were hardly out of the building before the lawyer came in again to report his difficulties. I could not do anything. I asked him, however: Why did the Standard Oil Company of New York send $1,000,000 over here in December, 1933, to aid the Germans in making gasoline from soft coal for war emergencies? Why do the International Harvester people continue to manufacture in Germany when their company gets nothing out of the country and when it has failed to collect its war losses? He saw my point and agreed that it looked foolish and that it only means greater losses if another war breaks loose.*[10]

The alliance between Nazi political power and American "Big Business" may well have looked foolish to Ambassador Dodd and the

American attorney he questioned. In practice, of course, "Big Business" is anything but foolish when it comes to promoting its own self-interest. Investment in Nazi Germany (along with similar investments in the Soviet Union) was a reflection of higher policies, with much more than immediate profit at stake, even though profits could not be repatriated. To trace these "higher policies" one has to penetrate the financial control of multinational corporations, because those who control the flow of finance ultimately control the day-to-day policies.

Carroll Quigley[11] has shown that the apex of this international financial control system before World War II was the Bank for International Settlements, with representatives from the international banking firms of Europe and the United States, in an arrangement that continued throughout World War II. During the Nazi period, Germany's representative at the Bank for International Settlements was Hitler's financial genius and president of the Reichsbank, Hjalmar Horace Greeley Schacht

Hjalmar Horace Greeley Schacht

Wall Street involvement with Hitler's Germany highlights two Germans with Wall Street connections — Hjalmar Schacht and "Putzi" Hanfstaengl. The latter was a friend of Hitler and Roosevelt who played a suspiciously prominent role in the incident that brought Hitler to the peak of dictatorial power — the Reichstag fire of 1933.[12]

The early history of Hjalmar Schacht, and in particular his role in the Soviet Union after the Bolshevik Revolution of 1917, was described in my earlier book, *Wall Street and the Bolshevik Revolution*. The elder Schacht had worked at the Berlin office of the Equitable Trust Company of New York in the early twentieth century. Hjalmar was born in Germany rather than New York only by the accident of his mother's illness, which required the family to return to Germany. Brother William Schacht was an American-born citizen. To record his American origins, Hjalmar's middle names were designated "Horace Greeley" after the well-know Democrat politician. Consequently, Hjalmar spoke fluent English and the post-war interrogation of Schacht in Project Dustbin was conducted in both German and English. The point to be made is that the Schacht family had its origins in New York, worked for the prominent Wall Street financial house of Equitable Trust (which was controlled by the Morgan firm), and throughout his life Hjalmar retained these Wall Street connections.[13] Newspapers and contemporary sources record repeated visits with Owen

Young of General Electric; Farish, chairman of Standard Oil of New Jersey; and their banking counterparts. In brief, Schacht was a member of the international financial elite that wields its power behind the scenes through the political apparatus of a nation. He is a key link between the Wall Street elite and Hitler's inner circle.

This book is divided into two major parts. Part One records the build-up of German cartels through the Dawes and Young Plans in the 1920s. These cartels were the major supporters of Hitler and Naziism and were directly responsible for bringing the Nazis to power in 1933. The roles of American I. G. Farben, General Electric, Standard Oil of New Jersey, Ford, and other U.S. firms is outlined. Part Two presents the known documentary evidence on the financing of Hitler, complete with photographic reproduction of the bank transfer slips used to transfer funds from Farben, General Electric, and other firms to Hitler, through Hjalmar Horace Greeley Schacht.

PART ONE

WALL STREET BUILDS
NAZI INDUSTRY

CHAPTER ONE

Wall Street Paves the Way for Hitler

The Dawes Plan, adopted in August 1924, fitted perfectly into the plans of the German General Staff's military economists. (Testimony before United States Senate, Committee on Military Affairs, 1946.)

The post-World War II Kilgore Committee of the United States Senate heard detailed evidence from government officials to the effect that,

. . .when the Nazis came to power in 1933, they found that long strides had been made since 1918 in preparing Germany for war from an economic and industrial point of view.[1]

This build-up for European war both before and after 1933 was in great part due to Wall Street financial assistance in the 1920s to create the German cartel system, and to technical assistance from well-known American firms which will be identified later, to build the German Wehrmacht. Whereas this financial and technical assistance is referred to as "accidental" or due to the "short-sightedness" of American businessmen, the evidence presented below strongly suggests some degree of premeditation on the part of these American financiers. Similar and unacceptable pleas of "accident" were made on behalf of American financiers and industrialists in the parallel example of building the military power of the Soviet Union from 1917 onwards. Yet these American capitalists were willing to finance and subsidize the Soviet Union while the Vietnam war was underway, knowing that the Soviets were supplying the other side.

The contribution made by American capitalism to German war preparations before 1940 can only be described as phenomenal. It was certainly crucial to German military capabilities. For instance, in 1934 Germany produced domestically only 300,000 tons of natural petroleum products and less than 300,000 tons of synthetic gasoline; the balance was imported. Yet, ten years later in World War II, after transfer of the Standard Oil of New Jersey hydrogenation patents and technology to I. G. Farben (used to produce synthetic gasoline from coal), Germany produced about 6 ½ million tons of oil — of which 85 percent (5 ½ million tons) was synthetic oil using the Standard Oil hydrogenation process. Moreover, the control of synthetic oil output in Germany was held by the I. G. Farben subsidiary, Braunkohle-Benzin A. G., and this Farben cartel itself was created in 1926 with Wall Street financial assistance.

On the other hand, the general impression left with the reader by modern historians is that this American technical assistance was accidental and that American industrialists were innocent of wrongdoing. For example, the Kilgore Committee stated:

> *The United States accidentally played an important role in the technical arming of Germany. Although the German military planners had ordered and persuaded manufacturing corporations to install modern equipment for mass production, neither the military economists nor the corporations seem to have realized to the full extent what that meant. Their eyes were opened when two of the chief American automobile companies built plants in Germany in order to sell in the European market, without the handicap of ocean freight charges and high German tariffs. Germans were brought to Detroit to learn the techniques of specialized production of components, and of straight-line assembly. What they saw caused further reorganization and refitting of other key German war plants. The techniques learned in Detroit were eventually used to construct the dive-bombing Stukas . . . . At a later period I. G. Farben representatives in this country enabled a stream of German engineers to visit not only plane plants but others of military importance, in which they learned a great deal that was eventually used against the United States.[2]*

Following these observations, which emphasize the "accidental" nature of the assistance, it has been concluded by such academic writers as Gabriel Kolko, who is not usually a supporter of big business, that:

> *It is almost superfluous to point out that the motives of the American firms bound to contracts with German concerns were not pro-Nazi, whatever else they may have been.[3]*

Yet, Kolko to the contrary, analyses of the contemporary American business press confirm that business journals and newspapers were fully aware of the Nazi threat and its nature, while warning their business readers of German war preparations. And even Kolko admits that:

> *The business press [in the United States] was aware, from 1935 on, that German prosperity was based on war preparations. More important, it was conscious of the fact that German industry was under the control of the Nazis and was being directed to serve Germany's rearmament, and the firm mentioned most frequently in this context was the giant chemical empire, I. G. Farben.*[4]

Further, the evidence presented below suggests that not only was an influential sector of American business aware of the nature of Naziism, but for its own purposes aided Naziism wherever possible (and profitable) — *with full knowledge that the probable outcome would be war involving Europe and the United States.* As we shall see, the pleas of innocence do not accord with the facts.

1924: The Dawes Plan

The Treaty of Versailles after World War I imposed a heavy reparations burden on defeated Germany. This financial burden — a real cause of the German discontent that led to acceptance of Hitlerism — was utilized by the international bankers for their own benefit. The opportunity to float profitable loans for German cartels in the United States was presented by the Dawes Plan and later the Young Plan. Both plans were engineered by these central bankers, who manned the committees for their own pecuniary advantages, and although technically the committees were not appointed by the U.S. Government, the plans were in fact approved and sponsored by the Government.

Post-war haggling by financiers and politicians fixed German reparations at an annual fee of 132 billion gold marks. This was about one quarter of Germany's total 1921 exports. When Germany was unable to make these crushing payments, France and Belgium occupied the Ruhr to take by force what could not be obtained voluntarily. In 1924 the Allies appointed a committee of bankers (headed by American banker Charles G. Dawes) to develop a program of reparations payments. The resulting Dawes Plan was, according to Georgetown University Professor of Inter-

national Relations Carroll Quigley, "largely a J. P. Morgan production."[5]
The Dawes Plan arranged a series of foreign loans totalling $800 million
with their proceeds flowing to Germany. These loans are important for our
story because the proceeds, raised for the greater part in the United States
from dollar investors, were utilized in the mid-1920s to create and consolidate the gigantic chemical and steel combinations of I. G. Farben and
Vereinigte Stahlwerke, respectively. These cartels not only helped Hitler
to power in 1933; they also produced the bulk of key German war materials used in World War II.

Between 1924 and 1931, under the Dawes Plan and the Young Plan,
Germany paid out to the Allies about 36 billion marks in reparations. At
the same time Germany borrowed abroad, mainly in the U.S., about 33
billion marks — thus making a net German payment of only three billion
marks for reparations. Consequently, the burden of German monetary
reparations to the Allies was actually carried by foreign subscribers to
German bonds issued by Wall Street financial houses — at significant profits for themselves, of course. And, let it be noted, these firms were owned
by the same financiers who periodically took off their banker hats and
donned new ones to become "statesmen." As "statesmen" they formulated the Dawes and Young Plans to "solve" the "problem" of
reparations. As bankers, they floated the loans. As Carroll Quigley points
out,

> *It is worthy of note that this system was set up by the inter-*
> *national bankers and that the subsequent lending of other*
> *people's money to Germany was very profitable to these*
> *bankers.*[6]

Who were the New York international bankers who formed these
reparations commissions?

The 1924 Dawes Plan experts from the United States were banker
Charles Dawes and Morgan representative Owen Young, who was president of the General Electric Company. Dawes was chairman of the Allied
Committee of Experts in 1924. In 1929 Owen Young became chairman of
the Committee of Experts, supported by J. P. Morgan himself, with alter-
nates T. W. Lamont, a Morgan partner, and T. N. Perkins, a banker with
Morgan associations. In other words, the U.S. delegations were purely and
simply, as Quigley has pointed out, J. P. Morgan delegations using the
authority and seal of the United States to promote financial plans for their
own pecuniary advantage. As a result, as Quigley puts it, the "international bankers sat in heaven, under a rain of fees and commissions."[7]

The German members of the Committee of Experts were equally interesting. In 1924 Hjalmar Schacht was president of the Reichsbank and had taken a prominent role in organization work for the Dawes Plan; so did German banker Carl Melchior. One of the 1928 German delegates was A. Voegler of the German steel cartel Stahlwerke Vereinigte. In brief, the two significant countries involved — the United States and Germany — were represented by the Morgan bankers on one side and Schacht and Voegler on the other, both of whom were key characters in the rise of Hitler's Germany and subsequent German rearmament.

Finally, the members and advisors of the Dawes and Young Commissions were not only associated with New York financial houses but, as we shall later see, were directors of firms within the German cartels which aided Hitler to power.

1928: The Young Plan

According to Hitler's financial genie, Hjalmar Horace Greeley Schacht, and Nazi industrialist Fritz Thyssen, it was the 1928 Young Plan (the successor to the Dawes Plan), formulated by Morgan agent Owen D. Young, that brought Hitler to power in 1933.

Fritz Thyssen claims that,

> *I turned to the National Socialist party only after I became convinced that the fight against the Young Plan was unavoidable if complete collapse of Germany was to be prevented.*[8]

The difference between the Young Plan and the Dawes Plan was that, while the Young Plan required payments in goods produced in Germany financed by foreign loans, the Young Plan required monetary payments and "In my judgment [wrote Thyssen] the financial debt thus created was bound to disrupt the entire economy of the Reich."

The Young Plan was assertedly a device to occupy Germany with American capital and pledge German real assets for a gigantic mortgage held in the United States. It is noteworthy that German firms with U.S. affiliations evaded the Plan by the device of temporary foreign ownership. For instance, A.E.G. (German General Electric), affiliated with General Electric in the U.S., was sold to a Franco-Belgian holding company and evaded the conditions of the Young Plan. It should be noted in passing that Owen Young was the major financial backer for Franklin D. Roosevelt in the United European venture when FDR, as a budding Wall

Street financier, endeavoured to take advantage of Germany's 1923 hyper-inflation. The United European venture was a vehicle to speculate and to profit upon the imposition of the Dawes Plan, and is clear evidence of private financiers (including Franklin D. Roosevelt) using the power of the state to advance their own interests by manipulating foreign policy.

Schacht's parallel charge that Owen Young was responsible for the rise of Hitler, while obviously self-serving, is recorded in a U.S. Government Intelligence report relating the interrogation of Dr. Fritz Thyssen in September, 1945:

> *The acceptance of the Young Plan and its financial principles increased unemployment more and more, until about one million were unemployed. People were desperate. Hitler said he would do away with unemployment. The government in power at that time was very bad, and the situation of the people was getting worse. That really was the reason of the enormous success Hitler had in the election. When the last election came, he got about 40%.*[9]

However, it was Schacht, not Owen Young, who conceived the idea which later became the Bank for International Settlements. The actual details were worked out at a conference presided over by Jackson Reynolds, "one of the leading New York bankers," together with Melvin Traylor of the First National Bank of Chicago, Sir Charles Addis, formerly of the Hong Kong and Shanghai Banking Corporation, and various French and German bankers.[10] The B.I.S. was essential under the Young Plan as a means to afford a ready instrument for promoting international financial relations. According to his own statements, Schacht also gave Owen Young the idea that later became the post-World War II International Bank for Reconstruction and Development:

> "*A bank of this kind will demand financial co-operation between vanquished and victors that will lead to community of interests which in turn will give rise to mutual confidence and understanding and thus promote and ensure peace.*"
>
> *I can still vividly recall the setting in which this conversation took place. Owen Young was seated in his armchair puffing away at his pipe, his legs outstretched, his keen eyes fixed unswervingly on me. As is my habit when propounding such arguments I was doing a quiet steady "quarter-deck" up and*

down the room. When I had finished there was a brief pause.
Then his whole face lighted up and his resolve found utterance
in the words:
   "Dr. Schacht, you gave me a wonderful idea and I am going
to sell it to the world."[11]

B.I.S. — The Apex of Control

This interplay of ideas and cooperation between Hjalmar Schacht in
Germany and, through Owen Young, the J. P. Morgan interests in New
York, was only one facet of a vast and ambitious system of cooperation and
international alliance for world control. As described by Carroll Quigley,
this system was ". . . nothing less than to create a world system of financial control, in private hands, able to dominate the political system of each
country and the economy of the world as a whole."[12]
   This feudal system worked in the 1920s, as it works today, through
the medium of the private central bankers in each country who control the
national money supply of individual economies. In the 1920s and 1930s,
the New York Federal Reserve System, the Bank of England, the Reichsbank in Germany, and the Banque de France also more or less influenced
the political apparatus of their respective countries indirectly through control of the money supply and creation of the monetary environment. More
direct influence was realized by supplying political funds to, or withdraw-
ing support from, politicians and political parties. In the United States, for
example, President Herbert Hoover blamed his 1932 defeat on withdrawal
of support by Wall Street and the switch of Wall Street finance and influence to Franklin D. Roosevelt.
   Politicians amenable to the objectives of financial capitalism, and
academics prolific with ideas for world control useful to the international
bankers, are kept in line with a system of rewards and penalties. In the
early 1930s the guiding vehicle for this international system of financial
and political control, called by Quigley the "apex of the system," was the
Bank for International Settlements in Basle, Switzerland. The B.I.S. apex
continued its work during World War II as the medium through which the
bankers — who apparently were not at war with each other — continued a
mutually beneficial exchange of ideas, information, and planning for the
post-war world. As one writer has observed, war made no difference to the
international bankers:

> *The fact that the Bank possessed a truly international staff did, of course, present a highly anomalous situation in time of war. An American President was transacting the daily business of the Bank through a French General Manager, who had a German Assistant General Manager, while the Secretary-General was an Italian subject. Other nationals occupied other posts. These men were, of course, in daily personal contact with each other. Except for Mr. McKittrick [see infra] they were of course situated permanently in Switzerland during this period and were not supposed to be subject to orders of their government at any time. However, the directors of the Bank remained, of course, in their respective countries and had no direct contact with the personnel of the Bank. It is alleged, however, that H. Schacht, president of the Reichsbank, kept a personal representative in Basle during most of this time.[13]*

It was such secret meetings, ". . . meetings more secret than any ever held by Royal Ark Masons or by any Rosicrucian Order . . ."[14] between the central bankers at the "apex" of control that so intrigued contemporary journalists, although they only rarely and briefly penetrated behind the mask of secrecy.

Building the German Cartels

A practical example of international finance operating behind the scenes to build and manipulate politico-economic systems is found in the German cartel system. The three largest loans handled by the Wall Street international bankers for German borrowers in the 1920s under the Dawes Plan were for the benefit of three German cartels which a few years later aided Hitler and the Nazis to power. American financiers were directly represented on the boards of two of these three German cartels. This American assistance to German cartels has been described by James Martin as follows: "These loans for reconstruction became a vehicle for arrangements that did more to promote World War II than to establish peace after World War I."[15]

The three dominant cartels, the amounts borrowed and the Wall Street floating syndicate were as follows:

German Cartel	Wall Street Syndicate	Amount Issued
Allgemeine Elektrizitäts-Gesellschaft (A.E.G.) (German General Electric)	National City Co.	$35,000,000
Vereinigte Stahlwerke (United Steelworks)	Dillon, Read & Co.	$70,225,000
American I.G. Chemical (I.G. Farben)	National City Co.	$30,000,000

Looking at all the loans issued, it appears that only a handful of New York financial houses handled the German reparations financing. Three houses — Dillon, Read Co.; Harris, Forbes & Co.; and National City Company — issued almost three-quarters of the total face amount of the loans and reaped most of the profits:

Wall Street Syndicate Manager	Participation in German industrial issues in U.S. capital market	Profits on German loans*	Percent of total
Dillon, Read & Co.	$241,325,000	$2.7 million	29.2
Harris, Forbes & Co.	186,500,000	1.4 million	22.6
National City Co.	173,000,000	5.0 million	20.9
Speyer & Co.	59,500,000	0.6 million	7.2
Lee, Higginson & Co.	53,000,000	n.a.	6.4
Guaranty Co. of N.Y.	41,575,000	0.2 million	5.0
Kuhn, Loeb & Co.	37,500,000	0.2 million	4.5
Equitable Trust Co.	34,000,000	0.3 million	4.1
TOTAL	$826,400,000	$10.4 million	99.9

Source: See Appendix A
*Robert R. Kuczynski, *Bankers Profits from German Loans* (Washington, D.C.: Brookings Institution, 1932), p. 127.

After the mid-1920s the two major German combines of I.G. Farben and Vereinigte Stahlwerke dominated the chemical and steel cartel system created by these loans. Although these firms had a voting majority in the cartels for only two or three basic products, they were able — through control of these basics — to enforce their will throughout the cartel. I.G. Farben was the main producer of basic chemicals used by other combines making chemicals, so its economic power position cannot be measured only by its capacity to produce a few basic chemicals. Similarly, Vereinigte Stahlwerke, with a pig-iron capacity greater than that of all other German iron and steel producers combined, was able to exercise far more influence in the semi-finished iron and steel products cartel than its capacity for pig-iron production suggests. Even so the percentage output of these cartels for all products was significant:

Vereinigte Stahlwerke products	Percent of German total production in 1938
Pig iron	50.8
Pipes and tubes	45.5
Heavy plate	36.0
Explosives	35.0
Coal tar	33.3
Bar steel	37.1

I.G. Farben	Percent of German total production in 1937
Synthetic methanol	100.0
Magnesium	100.0
Chemical nitrogen	70.0
Explosives	60.0
Synthetic gasoline (high octane)	46.0 (1945)
Brown coal	20.0

Among the products that brought I. G. Farben and Vereinigte Stahlwerke into mutual collaboration were coal tar and chemical nitrogen, both of prime importance for the manufacture of explosives. I. G. Farben had a cartel position that assured dominance in the manufacture and sale of chemical nitrogen, but had only about one percent of the coking capacity of Germany. Hence an agreement was made under which Farben explosives subsidiaries obtained their benzol, toluol, and other primary coal-tar products on terms dictated by Vereinigte Stahlwerke, while Vereinigte Stahlwerke's explosives subsidiary was dependent for its

nitrates on terms set by Farben. Under this system of mutual collaboration and inter-dependence, the two cartels, I. G. Farben and
Vereinigte Stahlwerke, produced 95 percent of German explosives in
1937-8 on the eve of World War II. *This production was from capacity
built by American loans and to some extent by American technology.*

The I. G. Farben-Standard Oil cooperation for production of synthetic oil from coal gave the I. G. Farben cartel a monopoly of German
gasoline production during World War II. Just under one half of German
high octane gasoline in 1945 was produced directly by I. G. Farben and
most of the balance by its affiliated companies.

In brief, in synthetic gasoline and explosives (two of the very basic
elements of modern warfare), the control of German World War II output
was in the hands of two German combines created by Wall Street loans
under the Dawes Plan.

Moreover, American assistance to Nazi war efforts extended into
other areas.[17] The two largest tank producers in Hitler's Germany were
Opel, a wholly owned subsidiary of General Motors (controlled by the J. P.
Morgan firm), and the Ford A. G. subsidiary of the Ford Motor Company
of Detroit. The Nazis granted tax-exempt status to Opel in 1936, to enable
General Motors to expand its production facilities. General Motors
obligingly reinvested the resulting profits into German industry. Henry
Ford was decorated by the Nazis for *his* services to Naziism. (See p. 93.)
Alcoa and Dow Chemical worked closely with Nazi industry with numerous transfers of their domestic U.S. technology. Bendix Aviation, in which
the J. P. Morgan-controlled General Motors firm had a major stock interest, supplied Siemens & Halske A. G. in Germany with data on automatic
pilots and aircraft instruments. As late as 1940, in the "unofficial war,"
Bendix Aviation supplied complete technical data to Robert Bosch for aircraft and diesel engine starters and received royalty payments in return.

In brief, American companies associated with the Morgan-Rocke-
feller international investment bankers — not, it should be noted, the vast
bulk of independent American industrialists — were intimately related to
the growth of Nazi industry. It is important to note as we develop our story
that General Motors, Ford, General Electric, DuPont and the handful of
U.S. companies intimately involved with the development of Nazi Germany were — except for the Ford Motor Company — controlled by the
Wall Street elite — the J. P. Morgan firm, the Rockefeller Chase Bank and
to a lesser extent the Warburg Manhattan bank.[18] This book is not an
indictment of *all* American industry and finance. It is an indictment of the

"apex" — those firms controlled through the handful of financial houses, the Federal Reserve Bank system, the Bank for International Settlements, and their continuing international cooperative arrangements and cartels which attempt to control the course of world politics and economics.

CHAPTER TWO

The Empire of I.G. Farben

Farben was Hitler and Hitler was Farben. (Senator Homer
T. Bone to Senate Committee on Military Affairs, June 4, 1943.)

On the eve of World War II the German chemical complex of I. G.
Farben was the largest chemical manufacturing enterprise in the world,
with extraordinary political and economic power and influence within the
Hitlerian Nazi state. I. G. has been aptly described as "a state within a
state."

The Farben cartel dated from 1925, when organizing genius Hermann Schmitz (with Wall Street financial assistance) created the super-
giant chemical enterprise out of six already giant German chemical companies — Badische Anilin, Bayer, Agfa, Hoechst, Weiler-ter-Meer, and
Griesheim-Elektron. These companies were merged to become Internationale Gesellschaft Farbenindustrie A.G. — or I.G. Farben for short.
Twenty years later the same Hermann Schmitz was put on trial at Nuremburg for war crimes committed by the I. G. cartel. Other I. G. Farben
directors were placed on trial but the American affiliates of I. G. Farben
and the American directors of I. G. itself were quietly forgotten; the truth
was buried in the archives.

It is these U.S. connections in Wall Street that concern us. Without
the capital supplied by Wall Street, there would have been no I. G.
Farben in the first place and almost certainly no Adolf Hitler and World
War II.

German bankers on the Farben *Aufsichsrat* (the supervisory Board of
Directors)[1] in the late 1920s included the Hamburg banker Max Warburg, whose brother Paul Warburg was a founder of the Federal Reserve
System in the United States. Not coincidentally, Paul Warburg was also on
the board of American I. G., Farben's wholly owned U.S. subsidiary. In
addition to Max Warburg and Hermann Schmitz, the guiding hand in the

creation of the Farben empire, the early Farben *Vorstand* included Carl Bosch, Fritz ter Meer, Kurt Oppenheim and George von Schnitzler.[2] All except Max Warburg were charged as "war criminals" after World War II.

In 1928 the American holdings of I. G. Farben (*i.e.*, the Bayer Company, General Aniline Works, Agfa Ansco, and Winthrop Chemical Company) were organized into a Swiss holding company, I. G. Chemie (Internationale Gesellschaft fur Chemische Unternehmungen A. G.), controlled by I. G. Farben in Germany. In the following year these American firms merged to become American I. G. Chemical Corporation, later renamed General Aniline & Film. Hermann Schmitz, the organizer of I. G. Farben in 1925, became a prominent early Nazi and supporter of Hitler, as well as chairman of the Swiss I. G. Chemie and president of American I. G. The Farben complex both in Germany and the United States then developed into an integral part of the formation and operation of the Nazi state machine, the Wehrmacht and the S.S.

I. G. Farben is of peculiar interest in the formation of the Nazi state because Farben directors materially helped Hitler and the Nazis to power in 1933. We have photographic evidence (see page 60) that I.G. Farben contributed 400,000 RM to Hitler's political "slush fund." It was this secret fund which financed the Nazi seizure of control in March 1933. Many years earlier Farben had obtained Wall Street funds for the 1925 cartelization and expansion in Germany and $30 million for American I. G. in 1929, and had Wall Street directors on the Farben board. It has to be noted that these funds were raised and directors appointed years before Hitler was promoted as the German dictator.

The Economic Power of I. G. Farben

Qualified observers have argued that Germany could not have gone to war in 1939 without I. G. Farben. Between 1927 and the beginning of World War II, I.G. Farben doubled in size, an expansion made possible in great part by American technical assistance and by American bond issues, such as the one for $30 million offered by National City Bank. By 1939 I. G. acquired a participation and managerial influence in some 380 other German firms and over 500 foreign firms. The Farben empire owned its own coal mines, its own electric power plants, iron and steel units, banks, research units, and numerous commercial enterprises. There were over 2,000 cartel agreements between I. G. and foreign firms — including Standard Oil of New Jersey, DuPont, Alcoa, Dow Chemical, and others in the United States. The full story of I.G. Farben and its world-wide activities before World War II can never be known, as key German records were destroyed in 1945 in anticipation of Allied victory. However, one post-war investigation by the U.S. War Department concluded that:

> *Without I. G.'s immense productive facilities, its intense research, and vast international affiliations, Germany's prosecution of the war would have been unthinkable and impossible; Farben not only directed its energies toward arming Germany, but concentrated on weakening her intended victims, and this double-barreled attempt to expand the German industrial potential for war and to restrict that of the rest of the world was not conceived and executed "in the normal course of business." The proof is overwhelming that I. G. Farben officials had full prior knowledge of Germany's plan for world conquest and of each specific aggressive act later undertaken . . . .*[3]

Directors of Farben firms (*i.e.*, the "I. G. Farben officials" referred to in the investigation) included not only Germans but also prominent American financiers. This 1943 U.S. War Department report concluded that I.G.'s assignment from Hitler in the prewar period was to make Germany self-sufficient in rubber, gasoline, lubricating oils, magnesium, fibers, tanning agents, fats, and explosives. To fulfill this critical assignment, vast sums were spent by I.G. on processes to extract these war materials from indigenous German raw materials — in particular the plentiful German coal resources. Where these processes could not be developed in Germany they were acquired from abroad under cartel arrangements. For example, the process for iso-octane, essential for aviation fuels, was obtained from the United States,

> . . . *in fact entirely [from] the Americans and has become known to us in detail in its separate stages through our agreements with them [Standard Oil of New Jersey] and is being used very extensively by us.*[4]

The process for manufacturing tetra-ethyl lead, essential for aviation gasoline, was obtained by I. G. Farben from the United States, and in 1939 I.G. was sold $20 million of high-grade aviation gasoline by Standard Oil of New Jersey. Even before Germany manufactured tetra-ethyl lead by the American process it was able to "borrow" 500 tons from the Ethyl Corporation. This loan of vital tetra-ethyl lead was not repaid and

I.G. forfeited the $1 million security. Further, I.G. purchased large stocks of magnesium from Dow Chemical for incendiary bombs and stockpiled explosives, stabilizers, phosphorus, and cyanides from the outside world. In 1939, out of 43 major products manufactured by I.G., 28 were of "primary concern" to the German armed forces. Farben's ultimate control of the German war economy, acquired during the 1920s and 1930s with Wall Street assistance, can best be assessed by examining the percentage of German war material output produced by Farben plants in 1943. Farben at that time produced 100 percent of German synthetic rubber, 95 percent of German poison gas (including all the Zyklon B gas used in the concentration camps), 90 percent of German plastics, 88 percent of German magnesium, 84 percent of German explosives, 70 percent of German gunpowder, 46 percent of German high octane (aviation) gasoline, and 33 percent of German synthetic gasoline.[5] (See Chart 2-1 and Table 2-1.)

Table 2-1: German Army (Wehrmacht) Dependence on I.G. Farben Production (1943):

Product	Total German Production	Percent Produced by I.G. Farben
Synthetic Rubber	118,600 tons	100
Methanol	251,000 tons	100
Lubricating Oil	60,000 tons	100
Dyestuffs	31,670 tons	98
Poison Gas	—	95
Nickel	2,000 tons	95
Plastics	57,000 tons	90
Magnesium	27,400 tons	88
Explosives	221,000 tons	84
Gunpowder	210,000 tons	70
High Octane (Aviation) Gasoline	650,000 tons	46
Sulfuric Acid	707,000 tons	35

Dr. von Schnitzler, of the I.G. Farben *Aufsichsrat*, made the following pertinent statement in 1943:

> *It is no exaggeration to say that without the services of German chemistry performed under the Four Year Plan the prosecution of modern war would have been unthinkable.*[6]

Unfortunately, when we probe the technical origins of the more important of these military materials — quite apart from financial support for Hitler — we find links to American industry and to American businessmen. There were numerous Farben arrangements with American firms, including cartel marketing arrangements, patent agreements, and technical exchanges as exemplified in the Standard Oil-Ethyl technology transfers mentioned above. These arrangements were used by I.G. to advance Nazi policy abroad, to collect strategic information, and to consolidate a world-wide chemical cartel.

One of the more horrifying aspects of I.G. Farben's cartel was the invention, production, and distribution of the Zyklon B gas, used in Nazi concentration camps. Zyklon B was pure Prussic acid, a lethal poison produced by I.G. Farben Leverkusen and sold from the Bayer sales office through Degesch, an independent license holder. Sales of Zyklon B amounted to almost three-quarters of Degesch business; enough gas to kill 200 million humans was produced and sold by I.G. Farben. The Kilgore Committee report of 1942 makes it clear that the I.G. Farben directors had precise knowledge of the Nazi concentration camps and the use of I.G. chemicals. This prior knowledge becomes significant when we later consider the role of the American directors in I.G.'s American subsidiary. The 1945 interrogation of I.G. Farben director von Schnitzler reads:

Q. What did you do when they told you that I.G. chemicals was [sic] being used to kill, to murder people held in concentration camps?
A. I was horrified.
Q. Did you do anything about it?
A. I kept it for me [to myself] because it was too terrible. . . . I asked Muller-Cunradi is it known to you and Ambros and other directors in Auschwitz that the gases and chemicals are being used to murder people.
Q. What did he say?
A. Yes: it is known to all I.G. directors in Auschwitz.[7]

There was no attempt by I.G. Farben to halt production of the gases — a rather ineffective way for von Schnitzler to express any concern for human life, "because it was too terrible."

The Berlin N.W. 7 office of I.G. Farben was the key Nazi overseas espionage center. The unit operated under Farben director Max Ilgner, nephew of I.G. Farben president Hermann Schmitz. Max Ilgner and Hermann Schmitz were on the board of American I.G., with fellow directors Henry Ford of Ford Motor Company, Paul Warburg of Bank of Manhattan, and Charles E. Mitchell of the Federal Reserve Bank of New York.

The so-called statistics department of N.W. 7 (known as VOWI) was created in 1929 and evolved into the economic intelligence arm of the Welrmacht.

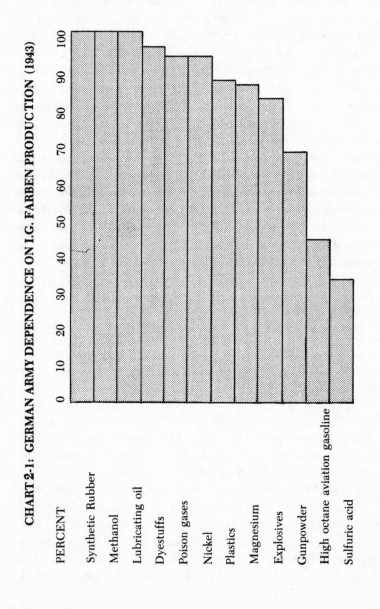

CHART 2-1: GERMAN ARMY DEPENDENCE ON I.G. FARBEN PRODUCTION (1943)

Source: Elimination of German Resources.

At the outbreak of war in 1939 VOWI employees were ordered into the Wehrmacht but in fact continued to perform the same work as when nominally under I.G. Farben. One of the more prominent of these Farben intelligence workers in N.W. 7 was Prince Bernhard of the Netherlands, who joined Farben in the early 1930s after completion of an 18-month period of service in the black-uniformed S.S.[8]

The U.S. arm of the VOWI intelligence network was Chemnyco, Inc. According to the War Department,

> *Utilizing normal business contacts Chemnyco was able to transmit to Germany tremendous amounts of material ranging from photographs and blueprints to detailed descriptions of whole industrial plants.*[9]

Chemnyco's vice president in New York was Rudolph Ilgner, an American citizen and brother of American I. G. Farben director Max Ilgner. In brief, Farben operated VOWI, the Nazi foreign intelligence operation, before World War II and the VOWI operation was associated with prominent members of the Wall Street Establishment through American I.G. and Chemnyco.

The U.S. War Department also accused I. G. Farben and its American associates of spearheading Nazi psychological and economic warfare programs through dissemination of propaganda via Farben agents abroad, and of providing foreign exchange for this Nazi propaganda. Farben's cartel arrangements promoted Nazi economic warfare — the outstanding example being the voluntary Standard Oil of New Jersey restriction on development of synthetic rubber in the United States at the behest of I. G. Farben. As the War Department report puts it:

> *The story in short is that because of Standard Oil's determination to maintain an absolute monopoly of synthetic rubber developments in the United States, it fully accomplished I.G.'s purpose of preventing United States production by dissuading American rubber companies from undertaking independent research in developing synthetic rubber processes.*[10]

In 1945 Dr. Oskar Loehr, deputy head of the I.G. "Tea Buro," confirmed that I. G. Farben and Standard Oil of New Jersey operated a "preconceived plan" to suppress development of the synthetic rubber industry in the United States, to the advantage of the German Wehrmacht and to the disadvantage of the United States in World War II.

Dr. Loehr's testimony reads (in part) as follows:

Q. Is it true that while the delay in divulging the buna [synthetic rubber] processes to American rubber companies was taking place, Chemnyco and Jasco were in the meantime keeping I.G. well informed in regard to synthetic rubber development in the U.S.?

A. Yes.

Q. So that at all times I.G. was fully aware of the state of the development of the American synthetic rubber industry?

A. Yes.

Q. Were you present at the Hague meeting when Mr. Howard [of Standard Oil] went there in 1939?

A. No.

Q. Who was present?

A. Mr. Ringer, who was accompanied by Dr. Brown of Ludwigshafen.

Q. Did they tell you about the negotiations?

A. Yes, as far as they were on the buna part of it.

Q. Is it true that Mr. Howard told I.G. at this meeting that the developments in the U.S. had reached such a stage that it would no longer be possible for him to keep the information in regard to the buna processes from the American companies?

A. Mr. Ringer reported it.

Q. Was it at that meeting that for the first time Mr. Howard told I.G. the American rubber companies might have to be informed of the processes and he assured I.G. that Standard Oil would control the synthetic rubber industry in the U.S.? Is that right?

A. That is right. That is the knowledge I got through Mr. Ringer.

Q. So that in all these arrangements since the beginning of the development of the synthetic rubber industry the suppression of the synthetic rubber industry in the U.S. was part of a preconceived plan between I.G. on the one hand and Mr. Howard of Standard Oil on the other?

A. That is a conclusion that must be drawn from the previous facts.[11]

I. G. Farben was pre-war Germany's largest earner of foreign exchange, and this foreign exchange enabled Germany to purchase strategic raw materials, military equipment, and technical processes, and to finance its overseas programs of espionage, propaganda, and varied military and political activities preceding World War II. Acting on behalf of the Nazi state, Farben broadened its own horizon to a world scale which maintained close relations with the Nazi regime and the Wehrmacht. A liaison office, the *Vermittlungsstelle W*, was established to maintain communications between I.G. Farben and the German Ministry of War:

The aim of this work is the building up of a tight organ-

ization for armament in the I.G. which could be inserted with-
out difficulty in the existing organization of the I.G. and the
individual plants. In the case of war, I.G. will be treated by the
authorities concerned with armament questions as one big plant
which, in its task for the armament, as far as it is possible to do so
from the technical point of view, will regulate itself without any
organizational influence from outside (the work in this direction
was in principle agreed upon with the Ministry of War
Wehrwirtschaftsant) *and from this office with the Ministry of*
Economy. To the field of the work of the Vermittlungsstelle W
belongs, besides the organizational set-up and long-range plan-
ning, the continuous collaboration with regard to the armament
and technical questions with the authorities of the Reich and
with the plants of the I.G.[12]

Unfortunately the files of the *Vermittlungsstelle* offices were de-
stroyed prior to the end of the war, although it is known from other sources
that from 1934 onwards a complex network of transactions evolved between I.G. and the Wehrmacht. In 1934 I. G. Farben began to mobilize
for war, and each I.G. plant prepared its war production plans and sub-
mitted the plans to the Ministries of War and Economics. By 1935-6 war
games were being held at I. G. Farben plants and wartime technical
procedures rehearsed.[13] These war games were described by Dr. Struss,
head of the Secretariat of I.G.'s Technical Committee:

> *It is true that since 1934 or 1935, soon after the estab-*
> *lishment of the* Vermittlungsstelle W *in the different works,*
> *theoretical war plant games had been arranged to examine how*
> *the effect of bombing on certain factories would materialize. It*
> *was particularly taken into consideration what would happen if*
> *100- or 500-kilogram bombs would fall on a certain factory and*
> *what would be the result of it. It is also right that the word*
> Kriegsspiele *was used for it.*
>
> *The* Kriegsspiele *were prepared by Mr. Ritter and Dr.*
> *Eckell, later on partly by Dr. von Brunning by personal order on*
> *Dr. Krauch's own initiative or by order of the Air Force, it is not*
> *known to me. The tasks were partly given by the* Vermittlung-
> sstelle W *and partly by officers of the Air Force. A number of*
> *officers of all groups of the Wehrmacht (Navy, Air Force, and*
> *Army) participated in these* Kriegsspiele.

*The places which were hit by bombs were marked in a map
of the plant so that it could be ascertained which parts of the
plant were damaged, for example a gas meter or an important
pipe line. As soon as the raid finished, the management of the
plant ascertained the damages and reported which part of the
plant had to stop working; they further reported what time
would be required in order to repair the damages. In a following
meeting the consequences of the Kriegsspiele were described
and it was ascertained that in the case of Leuna [plant] the
damages involved were considerably high; especially it was
found out that alterations of the pipe lines were to be made at
considerable cost.*[14]

Consequently, throughout the 1930s I. G. Farben did more than just
comply with orders from the Nazi regime. Farben was an initiator and
operator for the Nazi plans for world conquest. Farben acted as a research
and intelligence organization for the German Army and voluntarily
initiated Wehrmacht projects. In fact the Army only rarely had to
approach Farben; it is estimated that about 40 to 50 percent of Farben
projects for the Army were initiated by Farben itself. In brief, in the words
of Dr. von Schnitzler:

*Thus, in acting as it had done, I.G. contracted a great
responsibility and constituted a substantial aid in the chemical
domain and decisive help to Hitler's foreign policy, which led to
war and to the ruin of Germany. Thus, I must conclude that I.G.
is largely responsible for Hitler's policy.*

Polishing I. G. Farben's Public Image

This miserable picture of pre-war military preparation was known
abroad and had to be sold — or disguised — to the American public in
order to facilitate Wall Street fund-raising and technical assistance on
behalf of I. G. Farben in the United States. A prominent New York public
relations firm was chosen for the job of selling the I.G. Farben combine to
America. The most notable public relations firm in the late 1920s and
1930s was Ivy Lee & T.J. Ross of New York. Ivy Lee had previously undertaken a public relations campaign for the Rockefellers, to spruce up the
Rockefeller name among the American public. The firm had also
produced a syncophantic book entitled *USSR*, undertaking the same

clean-up task for the Soviet Union — even while Soviet labor camps were in full blast in the late 20s and early 30s.

From 1929 onwards Ivy Lee became public relations counsel for I. G. Farben in the United States. In 1934 Ivy Lee presented testimony to the House Un-American Activities Committee on this work for Farben.[15] Lee testified that I.G. Farben was affiliated with the American Farben firm and "The American I.G. is a holding company with directors such people as Edsel Ford, Walter Teagle, one of the officers of the City Bank . . . ." Lee explained that he was paid $25,000 per year under a contract made with Max Ilgner of I.G. Farben. His job was to counter criticism levelled at I.G. Farben within the United States. The advice given by Ivy Lee to Farben on this problem was acceptable enough:

> *In the first place, I have told them that they could never in the world get the American people reconciled to their treatment of the Jews: that that was just foreign to the American mentality and could never be justified in the American public opinion, and there was no use trying.*
>
> *In the second place, anything that savored of Nazi propaganda in this country was a mistake and ought not to be undertaken. Our people regard it as meddling with American affairs, and it was bad business.*[16]

The initial payment of $4,500 to Ivy Lee under this contract was made by Hermann Schmitz, chairman of I.G. Farben in Germany. It was deposited in the New York Trust Company under the name of I. G. Chemie (or the "Swiss I.G.," as Ivy Lee termed it). However, the second and major payment of $14,450 was made by William von Rath of the American I.G. and also deposited by Ivy Lee in New York Trust Company, for the credit of his personal account. (The firm account was at the Chase Bank.) This point about the origin of the funds is important when we consider the identity of directors of American I.G., because payment by American I.G. meant that the bulk of the Nazi propaganda funds were not of German origin. *They were American funds earned in the U.S. and under control of American directors, although used for Nazi propaganda in the United States.*

In other words, most of the Nazi propaganda funds handled by Ivy Lee were *not* imported from Germany.

The use to which these American funds were put was brought out under questioning by the House Un-American Activities Committee:

Mr. DICKSTEIN. As I understand you, you testified that you received no propaganda at all, and that you had nothing to do with the distribution of propaganda in this country?

Mr. LEE. I did not testify I received none Mr. Dickstein.

Mr. DICKSTEIN. I will eliminate that part of the question, then.

Mr. LEE. I testified that I disseminated none whatever.

Mr. DICKSTEIN. Have you received or has your firm received any propaganda literature from Germany at any time?

Mr. LEE. Yes, sir.

Mr. DICKSTEIN. And when was that?

Mr. LEE. Oh, we have received — it is a question of what you call propaganda. We have received an immense amount of literature.

Mr. DICKSTEIN. You do not know what that literature was and what it contained?

Mr. LEE. We have received books and pamphlets and newspaper clippings and documents, world without end.

Mr. DICKSTEIN. I assume someone in your office would go over them and see what they were?

Mr. LEE. Yes, sir.

Mr. DICKSTEIN. And then after you found out what they were, I assume you kept copies of them?

Mr. LEE. In some cases, yes: and in some, no. A great many of them, of course, were in German, and I had what my son sent me. He said they were interesting and significant, and those I had translated or excerpts of them made.[17]

Finally, Ivy Lee employed Burnham Carter to study American newspaper reports on Germany and prepare suitable pro-Nazi replies. It should be noted that this German literature was not Farben literature, it was official Hitler literature:

Mr. DICKSTEIN. In other words, you receive this material that deals with German conditions today. You examine it and you advise them. It has nothing to do with the German Government, although the material, the literature, is official literature of the Hitler regime. That is correct, is it not?

Mr. LEE. Well, a good deal of the literature was not official.

Mr. DICKSTEIN. It was not I.G. literature, was it?

Mr. LEE. No; I.G. sent it to me.

Mr. DICKSTEIN. Can you show us one scrap of paper that came in here that had anything to do with the I.G.?

Mr. LEE. Oh, yes. They issue a good deal of literature. But I do not want to beg the question. There is no question whatever that under their authority I have received an immense amount of material that came from official and unofficial sources.

Mr. DICKSTEIN. Exactly. In other words, the material that was sent here by the I.G. was material spread — we would call it propaganda — by authority of the German Government. But the distinction that you make in your statement is, as I take it, that the German Government did not send it to you directly; that it was sent to you by the I.G.

Mr. LEE. Right.

Mr. DICKSTEIN. And it had nothing to do with their business relations just now.

Mr. LEE. That is correct.

The American I.G. Farben

Who were the prominent Wall Street establishment financiers who directed the activities of American I.G., the I.G. Farben affiliate in the United States promoting Nazi propaganda?

American I.G. Farben directors included some of the more prominent members of Wall Street. German interests re-entered the United States after World War I, and successfully overcame barriers designed to keep I.G. out of the American market. Neither seizure of German patents, establishment of the Chemical Foundation, nor high tariff walls were a major problem.

By 1925, General Dyestuff Corporation was established as the exclusive selling agent for products manufactured by Gasselli Dyestuff (renamed General Aniline Works, Inc., in 1929) and imported from Germany. The stock of General Aniline Works was transferred in 1929 to American I.G. Chemical Corporation and later in 1939 to General Aniline & Film Corporation, into which American I.G. and General Aniline Works were merged. American I.G. and its successor, General Aniline & Film, is the unit through which control of I.G.'s enterprises in the U.S. was maintained. The stock authorization of American I.G. was 3,000,000 common A shares and 3,000,000 common B shares. In return for stock interests in General Aniline Works and Agfa-Ansco Corporation, I.G. Farben in Germany received all the B shares and 400,000 A shares. Thirty million dollars of convertible bonds were sold to the American public and guaranteed as to principal and interest by the German I.G. Farben, which received an option to purchase an additional 1,000,000 A shares.

Table 2-2: The Directors of American I.G. at 1930:

American I.G. Director	Citizenship	Other Major Associations
Carl BOSCH	German	FORD MOTOR CO. A-G
Edsel B. FORD	U.S.	FORD MOTOR CO. DETROIT
Max ILGNER	German	Directed I.G. FARBEN N.W.7 (INTELLIGENCE) office. Guilty at Nuremberg War Crimes Trials.
F. Ter MEER	German	Guilty at Nuremberg War Crimes Trials
H.A. METZ	U.S.	Director of I.G. Farben Germany and BANK OF MANHATTAN (U.S.)
C.E. MITCHELL	U.S.	Director of FEDERAL RESERVE BANK OF N.Y. and NATIONAL CITY BANK
Herman SCHMITZ (President)	German	On boards of I.G. Farben (Germany) Deutsche Bank (Germany) and BANK FOR INTERNATIONAL SETTLEMENTS. Guilty at Nuremberg War Crimes Trials.
Walter TEAGLE	U.S.	Director FEDERAL RESERVE BANK OF NEW YORK and STANDARD OIL OF NEW JERSEY
W.H. von RATH	Naturalized U.S.	Director of GERMAN GENERAL ELECTRIC (A.E.G.)
Paul M. WARBURG	U.S.	First member of the FEDERAL RESERVE BANK OF NEW YORK and BANK OF MANHATTAN
W.E. WEISS	U.S.	Sterling Products

Source: Moody's Manual of Investments; 1930, p. 2149.
Note: Walter DUISBERG (U.S.), W. GRIEF (U.S.), and Adolf KUTTROFF (U.S.) were also Directors of American I.G. Farben at this period.

The management of American I.G. (later General Aniline) was dominated by I.G. or former I.G. officials. (See Table 2-2.) Hermann Schmitz served as president from 1929 to 1936 and was then succeeded by his brother, Dietrich A. Schmitz, a naturalized American citizen, until 1941. Hermann Schmitz, who was also a director of the bank for International Settlements, the "apex" of the international financial control system. He remained as chairman of the board of directors from 1936 to 1939.

The original board of directors included nine members who were, or had been, members of the board of I.G. Farben in Germany (Hermann Schmitz, Carl Bosch, Max Ilgner, Fritz ter Meer, and Wilfred Grief), or had been previously employed by I.G. Farben in Germany (Walter Duisberg, Adolph Kuttroff, W.H. von Rath, Herman A. Metz). Herman A. Metz was an American citizen, a staunch Democrat in politics and a former comptroller of the City of New York. A tenth, W.E. Weiss, had been under contract to I.G.

Directors of American I.G. were not only prominent in Wall Street and American industry but more significantly were drawn from a few highly influential institutions:

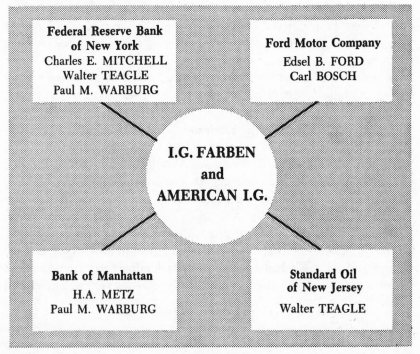

Federal Reserve Bank of New York
Charles E. MITCHELL
Walter TEAGLE
Paul M. WARBURG

Ford Motor Company
Edsel B. FORD
Carl BOSCH

I.G. FARBEN and AMERICAN I.G.

Bank of Manhattan
H.A. METZ
Paul M. WARBURG

Standard Oil of New Jersey
Walter TEAGLE

The remaining four members of the American I.G. board were promi nent American citizens and members of the Wall Street financial elite: C.E. Mitchell, chairman of National City Bank and the Federal Reserve Bank of New York; Edsel B. Ford, president of Ford Motor Company; W.C. Teagle, another director of Standard Oil of New Jersey; and, Paul Warburg, first member of the Federal Reserve Bank of New York and chairman of the Bank of Manhattan Company.

Directors of American I.G. were not only prominent in Wall Street and American industry but more significantly were drawn from a few highly influential institutions. (See chart above.)

Between 1929 and 1939 there were changes in the make-up of the board of American I.G. The number of directors varied from time to time, although a majority always had I.G. backgrounds or connections, and the board never had less than four American directors. In 1939 — presumably looking ahead to World War II — an effort was made to give the board a more American complexion, but despite the resignation of Hermann Schmitz, Carl Bosch, and Walter Duisberg, and the appointment of seven new directors, seven members still belonged to the I.G. group. This I.G. predominance increased during 1940 and 1941 as American directors, including Edsel Ford, realized the political unhealthiness of I.G. and re-signed.

Several basic observations can be made from this evidence. First, the board of American I.G. had three directors from the Federal Reserve Bank of New York, the most influential of the various Federal Reserve Banks. American I.G. also had interlocks with Standard Oil of New Jersey, Ford Motor Company, Bank of Manhattan (later to become the Chase Manhattan), and A.E.G. (German General Electric). Second, three members of the board of this American I.G. were found guilty at Nurem-burg War Crimes Trials. These were the German, not the American, members. Among these Germans was Max Ilgner, director of the I.G. Farben N.W. 7 office in Berlin, *i.e.*, the Nazi pre-war intelligence office. If the directors of a corporation are collectively responsible for the activities of the corporation, then the American directors should also have been placed on trial at Nuremburg, along with the German directors — that is, if the purpose of the trials was to determine war guilt. Of course, if the purpose of the trials had been to divert attention away from the U.S. involvement in Hitler's rise to power, they succeeded very well in such an objective.

CHAPTER THREE

General Electric Funds Hitler

> *Among the early Roosevelt fascist measures was the*
> *National Industry Recovery Act (NRA) of June 16, 1933. The*
> *origins of this scheme are worth repeating. These ideas were first*
> *suggested by Gerard Swope of the General Electric Company*
> *... following this they were adopted by the United States*
> *Chamber of Commerce . . . .*(Herbert Hoover, *The Memoirs of*
> *Herbert Hoover: The Great Depression, 1929-1941,* New
> York: The Macmillan Company, 1952, p. 420)

The multi-national giant General Electric has an unparalleled role in twentieth-century history. The General Electric Company electrified the Soviet Union in the 1920s and 1930s, and fulfilled for the Soviets Lenin's dictum that "Socialism = electrification."[1] The Swope Plan, created by General Electric's one-time president Gerard Swope, became Franklin D. Roosevelt's New Deal, by a process deplored by one-time President Herbert Hoover and described in *Wall Street and FDR.*[2] There was a long-lasting, intimate relationship between Swope and Young of General Electric Company and the Roosevelt family, as there was between General Electric and the Soviet Union. In 1936 Senator James A. Reed of Missouri, an early Roosevelt supporter, became aware of Roosevelt's betrayal of liberal ideas and attacked the Roosevelt New Deal program as a "tyrannical" measure "leading to despotism, [and] sought by its sponsors under the communistic cry of 'Social Justice.' " Senator Reed further charged on the floor of the Senate that Franklin D. Roosevelt was a "hired man for the economic royalists" in Wall Street and that the Roosevelt family "is one of the largest stockholders in the General Electric Company."[3]

As we probe into behind-the-scenes German interwar history and the story of Hitler and Naziism, we find both Owen D. Young and Gerard Swope of General Electric tied to the rise of Hitlerism and the suppression of German democracy. That General Electric directors are to be found in each of these three distinct historical categories—*i.e.*, the development of the Soviet Union, the creation of Roosevelt's New Deal, and the rise of Hitlerism—suggests how elements of Big Business are keenly interested in the socialization of the world, for their own purposes and objectives, rather than the maintenance of the impartial market place in a free society.[4] General Electric profited handsomely from Bolshevism, from Roosevelt's New Deal socialism, and, as we shall see below, from national socialism in Hitler's Germany.

General Electric in Weimar Germany

Walter Rathenau was, until his assassination in 1922, managing director of Allgemeine Elekrizitäts Gesellschaft (A.E.G.), or German General Electric, and like Owen Young and Gerard Swope, his counterparts in the U.S., he was a prominent advocate of corporate socialism. Walter Rathenau spoke out publicly against competition and free enterprise. Why? Because both Rathanau and Swope wanted the protection and cooperation of the state for their own corporate objectives and profit. (But not of course for anybody else's objectives and profits.) Rathanau expressed their plea in *The New Political Economy*:

> *The new economy will, as we have seen, be no state or governmental economy but a private economy committed to a civic power of resolution which certainly will require state cooperation for organic consolidation to overcome inner friction and increase production and endurance.*[5]

When we disentangle the turgid Rathenau prose, this means that the power of the State was to be made available to private firms for their own corporate purposes, *i.e.*, what is popularly known as national socialism. Rathenau spoke out publicly against competition and free enterprise. inheritance."[6] Not their *own* wealth, so far as can be determined, but the wealth of others who lacked political pull in the State apparatus.

Owen D. Young of General Electric was one of the three U.S. dele-, gates to the 1923 Dawes Plan meeting which established the German reparations program. And in the Dawes and Young Plans we can see how some private firms were able to benefit from the power of the State. The largest single loans from Wall Street to Germany during the 1920s were reparations loans; it was ultimately the U.S. investor who paid for German reparations. The cartelization of the German electrical industry under A.E.G. (as well as the steel and chemical industries discussed in Chapters One and Two) was made possible with these Wall Street loans:

Date of Offering	Borrower	Managing Bank in the U.S.	Face Amount of Issue
Jan. 26, 1925	Allgemeine Elektrizitäts-Gesellschaft (A.E.G.)	National City Co.	$10,000,000
Dec. 9, 1925	Allgemeine Elektrizitäts-Gesellschaft A.E.G.)	National City Co.	10,000,000
May 22, 1928	Allgemeine Elektrizitäts-Gesellschaft (A.E.G.)	National City Co.	10,000,000
June 7, 1928	Allgemeine Elektrizitäts-Gesellschaft (A.E.G.)	National City Co.	5,000,000

In 1928, at the Young Plan reparations meetings, we find General Electric president Owen D. Young in the chair as the chief U.S. delegate, appointed by the U.S. government to use U.S. government power and prestige to decide international financial matters enhancing Wall Street and General Electric profits. In 1930 Owen D. Young, after whom the Young Plan for German reparations was named, became chairman of the Board of General Electric Company in New York City. Young was also chairman of the Executive Committee of Radio Corporation of America and a director of both German General Electric (A.E.G.) and Osram in Germany. Young also served on the boards of other major U.S. corporations, including General Motors, NBC, and RKO; he was a councilor of the National Industrial Conference Board, a director of the International Chamber of Commerce, and deputy chairman of the board of the Federal Reserve Bank of New York.

Gerard Swope was president and director of General Electric Company as well as French and German associated companies, including A.E.G. and Osram in Germany. Swope was also a director of RCA, NBC, and the National City Bank of New York. Other directors of International General Electric at this time reflect Morgan control of the company, and both Young and Swope were generally known as the Morgan representatives on the G.E. board, which included Thomas Cochran, another partner in the J.P. Morgan firm. General Electric director Clark Haynes Minor was president of International General Electric in the 1920s. Another director was Victor M. Cutter of the First National Bank of Boston and a figure in the "Banana Revolutions" in Central America.

In the late 1920s Young, Swope, and Minor of International General Electric moved into the German electrical industry and gained, if not control as some have reported, then at least a substantial say in the internal affairs of both A.E.G. and Osram. In July 1929 an agreement was reached between General Electric and three German firms — A.E.G., Siemens & Halske, and Koppel and Company — which between them owned all the shares in Osram, the electric bulb manufacturer. General Electric purchased 16⅔ percent of Osram stock and reached a joint agreement for international control of electric bulbs production and marketing. Clark Minor and Gerard Swope became directors of Osram.[7]

In July 1929 great interest was shown in rumors circulating in German financial circles that General Electric was also buying into A.E.G. and that talks to this end were in progress between A.E.G. and G.E.[8] In August it was confirmed that 14 million marks of common A.E.G. stock were to be issued to General Electric. These shares, added to shares bought on the open market, gave General Electric a 25-percent interest in A.E.G. A closer working agreement was signed between the two companies, providing the German company U.S. technology and patents. It was emphasized in the news reports that A.E.G. would not have participation in G.E., but that on the other hand G.E. would finance expansion of A.E.G. in Germany.[9] The German financial press also noted that there was no A.E.G. representation on the board of G.E. in the United States but that five Americans were now on the board of A.E.G. The *Vossische Zeitung* recorded,

> *The American electrical industry has conquered the world,*
> *and only a few of the remaining opposing bastions have been*
> *able to withstand the onslaught* . . . .[10]

By 1930, unknown to the German financial press, General Electric had similarly gained an effective technical monopoly of the Soviet electrical industry and was soon to penetrate even the remaining bastions in Germany, particularly the Siemens group. In January 1930 three G.E. men were elected to the board of A.E.G. — Clark H. Minor, Gerard Swope, and E. H. Baldwin — and International General Electric (I.G.E.) continued its moves to merge the world electrical industry into a giant cartel under Wall Street control.

In February General Electric focused on the remaining German electrical giant, Siemens & Halske, and while able to obtain a large block of debentures issued on behalf of the German firm by Dillon, Read of New York, G.E. was not able to gain participation or directors on the Siemens board. While the German press recognized even this limited control as "an historical economic event of the first order and an important step toward a future world electric trust,"[11] Siemens retained its independence from General Electric — and this independence is important for our story. The *New York Times* reported,

> *The entire press emphasizes the fact that Siemens, contrary to A.E.G., maintains its independence for the future and points out that no General Electric representative will sit on Siemen's board of directors.*[12]

There is no evidence that Siemens, either through Siemens & Halske or Siemens-Schukert, participated directly in the financing of Hitler. Siemens contributed to Hitler only slightly and indirectly through a share participation in Osram. On the other hand, both A.E.G. and Osram directly financed Hitler through the Nationale Treuhand in substantial ways. Siemens retained its independence in the early 1930s while both A.E.G. and Osram were under American dominance and with American directors. *There is no evidence that Siemens, without American directors, financed Hitler. On the other hand, we have irrefutable documentary evidence (see page 56) that both German General Electric and Osram, both with American directors, financed Hitler.*

In the months following the attempted Wall Street take over of Siemens, the pattern of a developing world trust in the electrical industry clarified; there was an end to international patent fights and the G.E. interest in A.E.G. increased to nearly 30 percent.[13]

Consequently, in the early 1930s, as Hitler prepared to grab dictatorial power in Germany—backed by some, but by no means all, German and American industrialists—the German General Electric (A.E.G.) was owned by International General Electric (about 30 percent), the Gesellschaft für Electrische Unternemungen (25 percent), and Ludwig Lowe (25 percent). International General Electric also had an interest of about 16 2/3rds percent in Osram, and an additional indirect influence in

Companies Linked to German General Electric through Common Directors:	Directors of German General Electric (A.E.G.)	Relationship of Linked Firm with Financing of Hitler:
Accumulatoran-Fabrik	Quandt Pfeffer	*Direct Finance, see p. 55*
Osram	Mamroth Peierls	*Direct Finance, see p. 57*
Deutschen Babcock-Wilcox	Landau	Not known
Vereinigte Stahlwerke	Wolff	*Direct Finance, see p. 57*
	Nathan Kirdorf Goldschmidt	
Krupp	Nathan Klotzbach	*Direct Finance, see p. 59*
I.G. Farben	Bucher Flechtheim von Rath	*Direct Finance, see p. 57*
Allianz u. Stuttgarten Verein	von Rath	Reported, but not substantiated
Phoenix	Wolff Fahrenhorst	see p. 57
Thyssen	Fahrenhorst	*Direct Finance, see p. 104*
Demag	Fahrenhorst Flick	see p. 57
Dynamit	Flechtheim	Through I.G. Farben
Gelsenkirchener Bergwerks	Kirdorf Flechtheim	*Direct Finance, see p. 57*
International General Electric	Young Swope Minor Baldwin	Through A.E.G., see p. 52
American I.G. Farben	von Rath	Through I.G. Farben see p. 47
International Bank (Amsterdam)	H. Furstenberg Goldschmidt	Not known

Osram through A.E.G. directors. On the board of A.E.G., apart from the four American directors (Young, Swope, Minor, and Baldwin), we find Pferdmenges of Oppenheim & Co. (another Hitler financier), and Quandt, who owned 75 percent of Accumlatoren-Fabrik, a major direct financier of Hitler. In other words, among the German board members of A.E.G. we find representatives from several of the German firms that financed Hitler in the 1920s and 1930s.

General Electric and the Financing of Hitler

The tap root of modern corporate socialism runs deep into the management of two affiliated multi-national corporations: General Electric Company in the United States and its foreign associates, including German General Electric (A.E.G.), and Osram in Germany. We have noted that Gerard Swope, second president and chairman of General Electric, and Walter Rathanau of A.E.G. promoted radical ideas for control of the State by private business interests.

From 1915 onwards International General Electric (I.G.E.), located at 120 Broadway in New York City, acted as the foreign investment, manufacturing, and selling organization for the General Electric Company. I.G.E. held interests in overseas manufacturing companies including a 25 to 30-percent holding in German General Electric (A.E.G.), plus holdings in Osram G.m.b.H. Kommanditgesellschaft, also in Berlin. These holdings gave International General Electric four directors on the board of A.E.G., and another director at Osram, and significant influence in the internal domestic policies of these German companies. The significance of this General Electric ownership is that A.E.G. and Osram were prominent suppliers of funds for Hitler in his rise to power in Germany in 1933. A bank transfer slip dated March 2, 1933 from A.E.G. to Delbrück Schickler & Co. in Berlin requests that 60,000 Reichsmark be deposited in the "Nationale Treuhand" (National Trusteeship) account for Hitler's use. This slip is reproduced on page 56.

I.G. Farben was the most important of the domestic financial backers of Hitler, and (as noted elsewhere) I.G. Farben controlled American I.G. Moreover, several directors of A.E.G. were also on the board of I.G. Farben—*i.e.*, Hermann Bucher, chairman of A.E.G. was on the I.G. Farben board; so were A.E.G. directors Julius Flechtheim and Walter von Rath. I.G. Farben contributed 30 percent of the 1933 Hitler National Trusteeship (or takeover) fund.

ALLGEMEINE ELEKTRICITÄTS-GESELLSCHAFT
FINANZVERWALTUNG

BERLIN NW 40, Friedrich-Karl-Ufer 2/4

Bankhaus
   Delbrück Schickler & Co.,
      B e r l i n W.8,
      Mauerstr. 61-65.

Betrifft   X

2.März 1933

Wir überweisen Ihnen per Reichsbankgirokonto

ℛ 60 000,-

(i.W.: Sechzigtausend Reichsmark)

zu Gunsten des bei Ihnen geführten Kontos: "Nationale Treuhand".

Hochachtungsvoll

ALLGEMEINE ELEKTRICITÄTS-GESELLSCHAFT

Antwort erbeten an **Finanzverwaltung**

Original transfer slip dated March 2, 1933 from German General Electric to Delbrück, Schickler Bank in Berlin, with instructions to pay 60,-000 RM to the "Nationale Treuhand" fund (administered by Hjalmar Schacht and Rudolph Hess) used to elect Hitler in March 1933.

Source: Nuremburg Military Tribunal, document No. 391-395.

Walter Fahrenhorst of A.E.G. was also on the board of Phoenix A-G, Thyssen A-G and Demag A-G—and all were contributors to Hitler's fund. Demag A-G contributed 50,000 RM to Hitler's fund and had a director with A.E.G. — the notorious Friedrich Flick, and early Hitler supporter, who was later convicted at the Nuremberg Trials. Accumulatoren Fabrik A-G was a Hitler contributor (25,000 RM, see page 60) with two directors on the A.E.G. board, August Pfeffer and Gunther Quandt. Quandt personally owned 75 percent of Accumulatoren Fabrik.

Osram Gesellschaft, in which International General Electric had a 16 2/3rds direct interest, also had two directors on the A.E.G. board: Paul Mamroth and Heinrich Pferls. Osram contributed 40,000 RM directly to the Hitler fund. The Otto Wolff concern, Vereinigte Stahlwerke A-G, recipient of substantial New York loans in the 1920s, had three directors on the A.E.G. board: Otto Wolff, Henry Nathan and Jakob Goldschmidt. Alfred Krupp von Bohlen, sole owner of the Krupp organization and an early supporter of Hitler, was a member of the Aufsichsrat of A.E.G. Robert Pferdmenges, a member of Himmler's Circle of Friends, was also a director of A.E.G.

In other words, almost all of the German directors of German General Electric were financial supporters of Hitler and associated not only with A.E.G. but with other companies financing Hitler.

Walter Rathenau[14] became a director of A.E.G. in 1899 and by the early twentieth century was a director of more than 100 corporations. Rathenau was also author of the "Rathenau Plan," which bears a remarkable resemblance to the "Swope Plan" — *i.e.*, FDR's New Deal but written by Swope of G.E. *In other words, we have the extraordinary coincidence that the authors of New Deal-like plans in the U.S. and Germany were also prime backers of their implementers: Hitler in Germany and Roosevelt in the U.S.*

Swope was chairman of the board of General Electric Company and International General Electric. In 1932 the American directors of A.E.G. were prominently connected with American banking and political circles as follows:

GERARD SWOPE   Chairman of International General Electric and president of General Electric Company, director of National City Bank (and other companies), director of A.E.G. and Osram in Germany. Author of FDR's New Deal and member of numerous Roosevelt organizations.

INTERNATIONAL GENERAL ELECTRIC AND ITS LINKS TO "NATIONALE TREUFUND" ADMINISTERED BY HJALMAR SCHACHT AND RUDOLF HESS

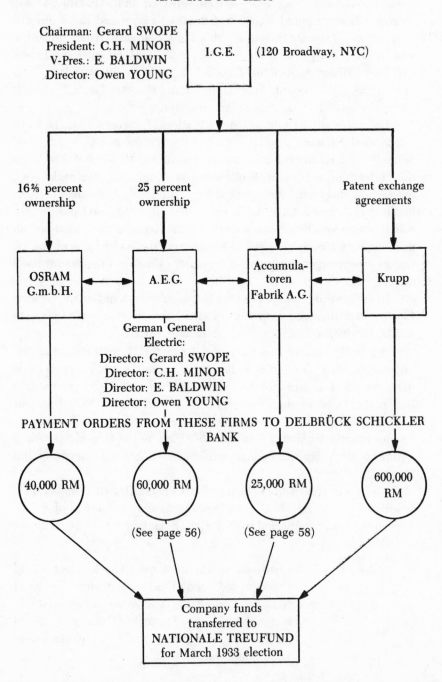

Chairman: Gerard SWOPE
President: C.H. MINOR
V-Pres.: E. BALDWIN
Director: Owen YOUNG

I.G.E.   (120 Broadway, NYC)

16⅔ percent ownership

25 percent ownership

Patent exchange agreements

OSRAM G.m.b.H.

A.E.G.

Accumula-toren Fabrik A.G.

Krupp

German General Electric:
Director: Gerard SWOPE
Director: C.H. MINOR
Director: E. BALDWIN
Director: Owen YOUNG

PAYMENT ORDERS FROM THESE FIRMS TO DELBRÜCK SCHICKLER BANK

40,000 RM

60,000 RM

25,000 RM

600,000 RM

(See page 56)

(See page 58)

Company funds transferred to
NATIONALE TREUFUND
for March 1933 election

OWEN D. YOUNG   Chairman of board of General Electric, and deputy chairman, Federal Reserve Bank of New York. Author, with J. P. Morgan, of the Young Plan which superseded the Dawes Plan in 1929. (See Chapter One.)

CLARK H. MINOR   President and director of International General Electric, director of British Thomson Houston, Compania Generale di Electtricita (Italy), and Japan Electric Bond & Share Company (Japan).

In brief, we have hard evidence of unquestioned authenticity (see p. 56) to show that German General Electric contributed substantial sums to Hitler's political fund. There were four American directors of A.E.G. (Baldwin, Swope, Minor, and Clark), which was 30 percent owned by International General Electric. Further, I.G.E. and the four American directors were the largest single interest and consequently had the greatest single influence in A.E.G. actions and policies. Even further, almost all other directors of A.E.G. were connected with firms (I. G. Farben, Accumulatoren Fabrik, *etc.*) which contributed directly — as firms — to Hitler's political fund. However, only the German directors of A.E.G. were placed on trial in Nuremburg in 1945.

Technical Cooperation with Krupp

Quite apart from financial assistance to Hitler, General Electric extended its assistance to cartel schemes with other Hitler backers for their mutual benefit and the benefit of the Nazi state. Cemented tungsten carbide is one example of this G.E.-Nazi cooperation. Prior to November 1928, American industries had several sources for both tungsten carbide and tools and dies containing this hard-metal composition. Among these sources were the Krupp Company of Essen, Germany, and two American firms to which Krupp was then shipping and selling, the Union Wire Die Corporation and Thomas Prosser & Son. In 1928 Krupp obligated itself to grant licenses under United States patents which it owned to the Firth-Sterling Steel Company and to the Ludlum Steel Company. Before 1928, this tungsten carbide for use in tools and dies sold in the United states for about $50 a pound.

The United States patents which Krupp claimed to own were

Zs./Boh.

Accumulatoren-Fabrik Aktiengesellschaft

HAUPTVERWALTUNG BERLIN SW 11, ASKANISCHER PLATZ 3

Drahtanschrift	Fernsprecher	Zahlstellen:
Tudorwerk Berlin	Ortsverkehr Sammel-Nr. B2 Lützow 4847	Postscheck-Konto Nr. 870 Berlin
	Fernverkehr Sammel-Nr. B2 Lützow 1331	Reichsbank-Giro-Konto Berlin
		Deutsche Bank und Disconto-Gesellschaft, Berlin W 8
		Berliner Handels-Gesellschaft, Berlin W 8

An das

Bankhaus Delbrück, Schickler & Co.,

B e r l i n, W. 8

Mauer Strasse 61/65

Direktion

Berlin SW 11, Askanischer Platz 3
Tag 9. März 1933.

Durch die Deutsche Bank, Berlin, überweisen wir Ihnen

einen Betrag von:

RM 25.000.— (i.W. Fünfundzwanzigtausend Reichsmark)

und bitten Sie, diesen Betrag dem bei Ihnen geführten Konto :

" Nationale Treuhand " gutzubringen.

Ihre Bestätigung bitten wir, an die Direktion unserer

Gesellschaft, auch auf dem Briefumschlag, zu richten.

Hochachtungsvoll

A c c u m u l a t o r e n - F a b r i k
A k t i e n g e s e l l s c h a f t

Herrn Schnelle
Zurück an Postbüro

Nr. 3100. A.L. 3000. 4. 32.

Original transfer slip dated March 9, 1933 from Accumulatoren-Fabrik to Delbrück, Schickler Bank in Berlin, with instructions to pay 25,-000 RM to the "Nationale Treuhand" fund, administered by Hjalmar Schacht and Rudolph Hess to elect Hitler in March 1933.

Gunther Quandt, the dominant shareholder (75 percent) of Accumulatoren, was also a director of German General Electric.

Source: Nuremburg Military Tribunal, document NI-391-395.

assigned from Osram Kommanditgesellschaft, and had been previously assigned by the Osram Company of Germany to General Electric. However, General Electric had also developed its own patents, principally the Hoyt and Gilson patents, covering competing processes for cemented tungsten carbide. General Electric believed that it could utilize these patents independently without infringing on or competing with Krupp patents. But instead of using the G.E. patents independently in competition with Krupp, or testing out its rights under the patent laws, General Electric worked out a cartel agreement with Krupp to pool the patents of both parties and to give General Electric a monopoly control of tungsten carbide in the United States.

The first step in this cartel arrangement was taken by Carboloy Company, Inc., a General Electric subsidiary, incorporated for the purpose of exploiting tungsten carbide. The 1920s price of around $50 a pound was raised by Carboloy to $453 a pound. Obviously, no firm could sell any great amounts of tungsten carbide in this price range, but the price would maximize profits for G.E. In 1934 General Electric and Carboloy were also able to obtain, by purchase, the license granted by Krupp to the Ludlum Steel Company, thereby eliminating one competitor. In 1936, Krupp was induced to refrain from further imports into the United States. Part of the price paid for the elimination from the American market of tungsten carbide manufactured abroad was a reciprocal undertaking that General Electric and Carboloy would not export from the U.S. Thus these American companies tied their own hands by contract, or permitted Krupp to tie their hands, and denied foreign markets to American industry. Carboloy Company then acquired the business of Thomas Prosser & Son, and in 1937, for nearly $1 million, Carboloy acquired the competing business of the Union Wire Die Corporation. By refusing to sell, Krupp cooperated with General Electric and Carboloy to persuade Union Wire Die Corporation to sell out.

Licenses to manufacture tungsten carbide were then refused. A request for license by the Crucible Steel Company was refused in 1936. A request by the Chrysler Corporation for a license was refused in 1938. A license by the Triplett Electrical Instrument Company was refused on April 25, 1940. A license was also refused to the General Cable Company. The Ford Motor Company for several years expressed strong opposition to the high-price policy followed by the Carboloy Company, and at one point made a request for the right to manufacture for its own use. This was refused. As a result of these tactics, General Electric and its subsidiary

Carboloy emerged in 1936 or 1937 with virtually a complete monopoly of tungsten carbide in the United States.

In brief, General Electric — with the cooperation of another Hitler supporter, Krupp — jointly obtained for G.E. a monopoly in the U.S. for tungsten carbide. So when World War II began, General Electric had a monopoly at an established price of $450 a pound — almost ten times more than the 1928 price — and use in the U.S. had been correspondingly restricted.

A.E.G. Avoids the Bombs in World War II

By 1939 the German electrical industry had become closely affiliated with two U.S. firms: International General Electric and International Telephone and Telegraph. The largest firms in German electrical production and their affiliations listed in order of importance were:

Firm and Type of Production	Percent of German 1939 production	U.S. Affiliated Firm
Heavy Current Industry		
General Electric (A.E.G.)	40 percent	International General Electric
Siemens Schukert A.G.	40 percent	None
Brown Boveri et Cie	17 percent	None
Telephone and Telegraph		
Siemens und Halske	60 percent	None
Lorenz A.G.	35 percent	I.T.T.
Radio		
Telefunken (A.E.G. after 1941)	60 percent	International General Electric
Lorenz	35 percent	I.T.T.
Wire and Cable		
Felton & Guilleaume A.G.	20 percent	I.T.T.
Siemens	20 percent	None
A.E.G.	20 percent	International General Electric

In other words, in 1939 the German electrical equipment industry was concentrated into a few major corporations linked in an international cartel and by stock ownership to two major U.S. corporations. This industrial complex was never a prime target for bombing in World War II. The A.E.G. and I.T.T. plants were hit only incidentally in area raids and then but rarely. The electrical equipment plants bombed as targets were not those affiliated with U.S. firms. It was Brown Boveri at Mannheim and Siemensstadt in Berlin — which were *not* connected with the U.S. — who were bombed. As a result, German production of electrical war equipment rose steadily throughout World War II, peaking as late as 1944. According to the U.S. Strategic Bombing Survey reports, "In the opinion of Speers' assistants and plant officials, the war effort in Germany was never hindered in any important manner by any shortage of electrical equipment."[15]

One example of the non-bombing policy for German General Electric was the A.E.G. plant at 135 Muggenhofer Strasse, Nuremburg. Study of this plant's output in World War II is of interest because it illustrates the extent to which purely peacetime production was converted to war work. The pre-war plant manufactured household equipment, such as hot plates, electric ranges, electric irons, toasters, industrial baking ovens, radiators, water heaters, kitchen ovens, and industrial heaters. In 1939, 1940 and 1941, most of the Nuremburg plant's production facilities were used for the manufacture of peacetime products. In 1942 the plant's production was shifted to manufacture of war equipment. Metal parts for communications equipment and munitions such as bombs and mines were made. Other war production consisted of parts for searchlights and amplifiers. The following tabulation very strikingly shows the conversion to war work:

Year	Total sales in 1000 RM	Percent for war	Percent ordinary production
1939	12,469	5	95
1940	11,754	15	85
1941	21,194	40	60
1942	20,689	61	39
1943	31,455	67	33
1944	31,205	69	31

I.G. FARBENINDUSTRIE AKTIENGESELLSCHAFT
Bankabteilung

POSTANSCHRIFT
I G Farbenindustrie Aktiengesellschaft
Bankabteilung
Frankfurt (Main) 20. Grüneburgplatz

DRAHTWORT
Igefarben
Frankfurtmain

FERNRUF
Ortsverkehr: Sammelnummer 200 27   8—17 Uhr
Fernverkehr : Sammelnummer 585 49   Sonnabend 8-13½ Uhr

GESCHÄFTSZEIT
8—17 Uhr

KONTEN
Reichsbank-Giro-Konto Frankfurt (Main)
Postscheck-Konto 241 Frankfurt (Main)

Firma

Delbrück Schickler & Co.,

B e r l i n W.8.

Mauerstr. 63/65.

Ihre Zeichen	Ihre Nachricht vom	Unsere Zeichen (bei Antwort anzugeben)	FRANKFURT (MAIN) 20
		B./G3.	den 27. Febr. 33.

Betreff

Wir teilen Ihnen hierdurch mit, dass wir die
DRESDNER BANK in FRANKFURT/M., FRANKFURT A/M., beauftragt
haben, Ihnen morgen vormittag

RM 400.000.--

zu vergüten, die Sie zu Gunsten des Kontos

» NATIONALE TREUHAND»

verwenden wollen.

Hochachtungsvoll

I.G. FARBENINDUSTRIE AKTIENGESELLSCHAFT.

dch. EILBOTEN.

Original transfer slip dated February 27, 1933 from I.G. Farben to Delbrück, Schickler Bank in Berlin with instructions to pay 4000,000 RM to the "Nationale Treuhand" fund (administered by Hjalmar Schacht and Rudolph Hess) used to elect Hitler in March 1933.

Source: Nuremburg Military Tribunal, document No. NI-391-395.

The actual physical damage by bombing to this plant was insignificant. No serious damage occurred until the raids of February 20 and 21, 1945, near the end of the war, and then protection had been fairly well developed. Raids during which bombs struck in the plant area and the trifling damage done are listed as follows:

Date of raid	Bombs striking plant	Damage done
March 8, 1943	30 stick type I.B.	Trifling, but 3 storehouses outside the main plant destroyed.
Sept. 9, 1944	None (blast damage)	Trifling, glass and blackout curtain damage.
Nov. 26, 1944	1-1000 lb. HE in open space in plant grounds	Wood shop destroyed, water main broken.
Feb. 20, 1945	2 HE	3 buildings damaged.
Feb. 21, 1945	5 HE, many I.B.'s	Administration bldg. destroyed & enameling works damaged by HE.

Another example of a German General Electric Plant not bombed is the A.E.G. plant at Koppelsdorf producing radar sets and bomber antennae. Other A.E.G. plants which were not bombed and their war equipment production were:

LIST OF A.E.G. FACTORIES NOT BOMBED IN WORLD WAR II

	Name of Branch	Location	Product
1.	Werk Reichmannsdorf mit Unterabteilungen in Wallendorf und Unterweissbach	Kries Saalfeld	Measuring Instruments
2.	Werk Marktschorgast	Bayreuth	Starters
3.	Werk F18ha	Sachsen	Short Wave Sending Sets
4.	Werk Reichenbach	Vogtland	Dry Cell Batteries
5.	Werk Burglengefeld	Sachsen/S.E. Chemnitz	Heavy Starters
6.	Werk Nuremburg	Belringersdorf/ Nuremburg	Small Components

7. Werk Zirndorf	Nuremburg	Heavy Starters
8. Werk Mattinghofen	Oberdonau	1 KW Senders 250 Meters & long wave for torpedo boats & U-boats
9. Unterwerk Neustadt	Coburg	Radar Equipment

That the A.E.G. plants in Germany were not bombed in World War II was confirmed by the United States Strategic Bombing Survey, officered by such academics as John K. Galbraith and such Wall Streeters as George W. Ball and Paul H. Nitze. Their "German Electrical Equipment Indus try Report" dated January 1947 concludes:

> *The industry has never been attacked as a basic target sys tem, but a few plants, i.e. Brown Boveri at Mannheim, Bosch at Stuutgart and Siemenstadt in Berlin, have been subjected to pre- cision raids; many others were hit in area raids.*[17]

At the end of World War II an Allied investigation team known as FIAT was sent to examine bomb damage to German electrical industry plants. The team for the electrical industry consisted of Alexander G.P.E. Sanders of International Telephone and Telegraph of New York, Whit- worth Ferguson of Ferguson Electric Company, New York, and Erich J. Borgman of Westinghouse Electric. Although the stated objective of these teams was to examine the effects on Allied bombing of German targets, the objective of this particular team was to get the German electrical equipment industry back into production as soon as possible. Whitworth Ferguson wrote a report dated March 31, 1945 on the A.E.G. Ostland- werke and concluded, "this plant is immediately available for produc- tion of fine metal parts and assemblies."[18]

To conclude, we find that both Rathenau of A.E.G. and Swope of General Electric in the U.S. had similar ideas of putting the State to work for their own corporate ends. General Electric was prominent in financing Hitler, it profited handsomely from war production — and yet it managed to evade bombing in World War II. Obviously the story briefly surveyed here deserves a much more thorough — and official — investigation.

CHAPTER FOUR
Standard Oil Fuels World War II

*In two years Germany will be manufacturing oil and gas
enough out of soft coal for a long war. The Standard Oil of New
York is furnishing millions of dollars to help.* (Report from the
Commercial Attaché, U.S. Embassy in Berlin, Germany, January
1933, to State Department in Washington, D.C.)

The Standard Oil group of companies, in which the Rockefeller family
owned a one-quarter (and controlling) interest,[1] was of critical assistance
in helping Nazi Germany prepare for World War II. This assistance in
military preparation came about because Germany's relatively insignificant supplies of crude petroleum were quite insufficient for modern
mechanized warfare; in 1934 for instance about 85 percent of German
finished petroleum products were imported. The solution adopted by Nazi
Germany was to manufacture synthetic gasoline from its plentiful
domestic coal supplies. It was the hydrogenation process of producing synthetic gasoline and iso-octane properties in gasoline that enabled Germany
to go to war in 1940—and this hydrogenation process was developed and
financed by the Standard Oil laboratories in the United States in
partnership with I.G. Farben.

Evidence presented to the Truman, Bone, and Kilgore Committees
after World War II confirmed that Standard Oil had at the same time
"seriously imperiled the war preparations of the United States."[2]
Documentary evidence was presented to all three Congressional committees that before World War II Standard Oil had agreed with I.G.
Farben, in the so-called Jasco agreement, that synthetic rubber was within
Farben's sphere of influence, while Standard Oil was to have an absolute
monopoly in the U.S. *only if and when* Farben allowed development of
synthetic rubber to take place in the U.S.:

Accordingly [concluded the Kilgore Committee] Standard fully accomplished I.G.'s purpose of preventing United States production by dissuading American rubber companies from undertaking independent research in developing synthetic rubber processes.[3]

Regrettably, the Congressional committees did not explore an even more ominous aspect of this Standard Oil—I.G. Farben collusion: that at this time directors of Standard Oil of New Jersey had not only strategic warfare affiliations to I.G. Farben, but had other links with Hitler's Germany—even to the extent of contributing, through German subsidiary companies, to Heinrich Himmler's personal fund and with membership in Himmler's Circle of Friends as late as 1944.

During World War II Standard Oil of New Jersey was accused of treason for this pre-war alliance with Farben, even while its continuing wartime activities within Himmler's Circle of Friends were unknown. The accusations of treason were vehemently denied by Standard Oil. One of the more prominent of these defenses was published by R.T. Haslam, a director of Standard Oil of New Jersey, in *The Petroleum Times* (December 25, 1943), and entitled "Secrets Turned into Mighty War Weapons Through I.G. Farben Agreement."[4] This was an attempt to turn the tables and present the pre-war collusion as advantageous to the United States.

Whatever may have been Standard Oil's wartime recollections and hasty defense, the 1929 negotiations and contracts between Standard and I.G. Farben were recorded in the contemporary press and describe the agreements between Standard Oil of New Jersey and I.G. Farben and their intent. In April 1929 Walter C. Teagle, president of Standard Oil of New Jersey, became a director of the newly organized American I.G. Farben. Not because Teagle was interested in the chemical industry but because,

It has for some years past enjoyed a very close relationship with certain branches of the research work of the I.G. Farbenindustrie which bear closely upon the oil industry.[5]

It was announced by Teagle that joint research work on production of oil from coal had been carried on for some time and that a research laboratory for this work was to be established *in the United States.*[6] In November 1929 this jointly owned Standard—Farben research company was established *under the management of the Standard Oil Company of New Jersey*, and all research and patents relating to production of oil from coal held by both I.G. and Standard were pooled. Previously, during the period 1926-1929, the two companies had cooperated in development of the hydrogenation process, and experimental plants had been placed in operation in both the U.S. and Germany. It was now proposed to erect new plants in the U.S. at Bayway, New Jersey and Baytown, Texas, in addition to expansion of the earlier experimental plant at Baton Rouge. Standard announced:

> . . . *the importance of the new contract as applied to this country lay in the fact that it made certain that the hydrogenation process would be developed commercially in this country under the guidance of American oil interests.*[7]

In December 1929 the new company, Standard I.G. Company, was organized. F.A. Howard was named president, and its German and American directors were announced as follows: E.M. Clark, Walter Duisberg, Peter Hurll, R.A. Reidemann, H.G. Seidel, Otto von Schenck, and Guy Wellman.

The majority of the stock in the research company was owned by Standard Oil. The technical work, the process development work, and the construction of three new oil-from-coal plants in the United States was placed in the hands of the Standard Oil Development Company, the Standard Oil technical subsidiary. It is clear from these contemporary reports that the development work on oil from coal was undertaken by Standard Oil of New Jersey within the United States, in Standard Oil plants and with majority financing and control by Standard. The results of this research were made available to I.G. Farben and became the basis for the development of Hitler's oil from-coal-program which made World War II possible.

The Haslam article, written by a former Professor of Chemical Engineering at M.I.T. (then vice president of Standard Oil of New Jersey) argued—contrary to these recorded facts—that Standard Oil was able, through its Farben agreements, to obtain *German* technology for the United States. Haslam cited the manufacture of toluol and paratone (Oppanol), used to stabilize viscosity of oil, an essential material for desert and Russian winter tank operations, and buna rubber. However, this article, with its erroneous self-serving claims, found its way to wartime Germany and became the subject of a "Secret" I.G. Farben memorandum dated

June 6, 1944 from Nuremburg defendent and then-Farben official von Knieriem to fellow Farben management officials. This von Knieriem "Secret" memo set out those facts Haslam avoided in his *Petroleum Times* article. The memo was in fact a summary of what Standard was unwilling to reveal to the American public—*i.e.*, the major contribution made by Standard Oil of New Jersey to the Nazi war machine. The Farben memorandum states that the Standard Oil agreements were *absolutely essential* for I.G. Farben:

> *The closing of an agreement with Standard was necessary for technical, commercial, and financial reasons:* technically, *because the specialized experience which was available only in a big oil company was necessary to the further development of our process,* and no such industry existed in Germany; commercially, *because in the absence of state economic control in Germany at that time, IG had to avoid a competitive struggle with the great oil powers, who always sold the best gasoline at the lowest price in contested markets;* financially, *because IG, which had already spent extraordinarily large sums for the development of the process,* had to seek financial relief in order to be able to continue development in other new technical fields, such as buna.[8]

The Farben memorandum then answered the key question: What did I.G. Farben acquire from Standard Oil that was "vital for the conduct of war?" The memo examines those products cited by Haslam—*i.e.*, iso-octane, tuluol, Oppanol-Paratone, and buna—and demonstrates that contrary to Standard Oil's public claim, their technology came to a great extent from the U.S., not from Germany.

On iso-octane the Farben memorandum reads, in part,

> *By reason of their decades of work on motor fuels, the Americans were ahead of us in their knowledge of the quality requirements that are called for by the different uses of motor fuels. In particular they had developed, at great expense, a large number of methods of testing gasoline for different uses. On the basis of their experiments they had recognized the good anti-knock quality of iso-octane long before they had any knowledge of our hydrogenation process. This is proved by the single fact that in America fuels are graded in octane numbers, and iso-octane was entered as the best fuel with the number 100. All this*

knowledge naturally became ours as a result of the agreement,
which saved us much effort and protected us against many
errors.

I.G. Farben adds that Haslam's claim that the production of iso-
octane became known in America only through the Farben hydrogenation
process was not correct:

> *Especially in the case of iso-octane, it is shown that we owe*
> *much to the Americans because in our own work we could draw*
> *widely on American information on the behavior of fuels in*
> *motors. Moreover, we were also kept currently informed by the*
> *Americans on the progress of their production process and its*
> *further development.*
>
> *Shortly before the war, a new method for the production of*
> *iso-octane was found in America — alkylation with isomerization*
> *as a preliminary step. This process, which Mr. Haslam does not*
> *mention at all, originates in fact entirely with the Americans and*
> *has become known to us in detail in its separate stages through*
> *our agreements with them, and is being used very extensively by*
> *us.*

On toluol, I.G. Farben points to a factual inaccuracy in the Haslam
article: toluol was *not* produced by hydrogenation in the U.S. as claimed
by Professor Haslam. In the case of Oppanol, the I.G. memo calls
Haslam's information "incomplete" and so far as buna rubber is concerned, "we never gave technical information to the Americans, nor did
technical cooperation in the buna field take place." Most importantly, the
Farben memo goes on to describe some products not cited by Haslam in
his article:

> *As a consequence of our contracts with the Americans, we*
> *received from them, above and beyond the agreement, many*
> *very valuable contributions for the synthesis and improvement*
> *of motor fuels and lubricating oils, which just now during the*
> *war are most useful to us; and we also received other advantages*
> *from them. Primarily, the following may be mentioned:*
>
> *(1) Above all, improvement of fuels through the addition of*
> tetraethyl-lead *and the manufacture of this product. It need not*
> *be especially mentioned that without tetraethyl-lead the present*
> *methods of warfare would be impossible. The fact that since the*

beginning of the war we could produce tetraethyl-lead is entirely due to the circumstances that, shortly before, the Americans had presented us with the production plans, complete with their know-how. It was, moreover, the first time that the Americans decided to give a license on this process in a foreign country (besides communication of unprotected secrets) and this only on our urgent requests to Standard Oil to fulfill our wish. Contractually we could not demand it, and we found out later that the War Department in Washington gave its permission only after long deliberation.

(2) Conversion of low-molecular unsaturates into usable gasoline (polymerization). Much work in this field has been done here as well as in America. But the Americans were the first to carry the process through on a large scale, which suggested to us also to develop the process on a large technical scale. But above and beyond that, plants built according to American processes are functioning in Germany.

(3) In the field of lubricating oils as well, Germany through the contract with America, learned of experience which is extraordinarily important for present day warfare.

In this connection, we obtained not only the experience of Standard, but, through Standard, the experiences of General Motors and other large American motor companies as well.

(4) As a further remarkable example of advantageous effect for us of the contract between IG and Standard Oil, the following should be mentioned: in the years 1934/1935 our government had the greatest interest in gathering from abroad a stock of especially valuable mineral oil products (in particular, aviation gasoline and aviation lubricating oil), and holding it in reserve to an amount approximately equal to 20 million dollars at market value. The German Government asked IG if it were not possible, on the basis of its friendly relations with Standard Oil, to buy this amount in Farben's name; actually, however, as trustee of the German Government. The fact that we actually succeeded by means of the most difficult negotiations in buying the quantity desired by our government from the American Standard Oil Company and the Dutch—English Royal—Dutch—Shell group and in transporting it to Germany, was made possible only through the aid of the Standard Oil Co.

Ethyl Lead for the Wehrmacht

Another prominent example of Standard Oil assistance to Nazi Germany—in cooperation with General Motors—was in supplying ethyl lead. Ethyl fluid is an anti-knock compound used in both aviation and automobile fuels to eliminate knocking, and so improve engine efficiency; without such anti-knocking compounds modern mobile warfare would be impractical.

In 1924 the Ethyl Gasoline Corporation was formed in New York City, jointly owned by the Standard Oil Company of New Jersey and General Motors Corporation, to control and utilize U.S. patents for the manufacture and distribution of tetraethyl lead and ethyl fluid in the U.S. and abroad. Up to 1935 manufacture of these products was undertaken *only* in the United States. In 1935 Ethyl Gasoline Corporation transferred its know-how to Germany for use in the Nazi rearmament program. This transfer was undertaken over the protests of the U.S. Government.

Ethyl's intention to transfer its anti-knock technology to Nazi Germany came to the attention of the Army Air Corps in Washington, D.C. On December 15, 1934 E. W. Webb, president of Ethyl Gasoline, was advised that Washington had learned of the intention of "forming a German company with the I.G. to manufacture ethyl lead in that country." The War Department indicated that there was considerable criticism of this technological transfer, which might "have the gravest repercussions" for the U.S.; that the commercial demand for ethyl lead in Germany was too small to be of interest; and,

> . . . *it has been claimed that Germany is secretly arming [and] ethyl lead would doubtless be a valuable aid to military aeroplanes.*[10]

The Ethyl Company was then advised by the Army Air Corps that "under no conditions should you or the Board of Directors of the Ethyl Gasoline Corporation disclose any secrets or 'know-how' in connection with the manufacture of tetraethyl lead to Germany."[11]

On January 12, 1935 Webb mailed to the Chief of the Army Air Corps a "Statement of Facts," which was in effect a denial that any such technical knowledge would be transmitted; he offered to insert such a clause in the contract to guard against any such transfer. However, contrary to its pledge to the Army Air Corps, Ethyl subsequently signed a joint production agreement with I.G. Farben in Germany to form Ethyl G.m.b.H. and with Montecatini in fascist Italy for the same purpose.

It is worth noting the directors of Ethyl Gasoline Corporation at the time of this transfer:[12] E.W. Webb, president and director; C.F. Kettering; R.P. Russell; W.C. Teagle, Standard Oil of New Jersey and trustee of FDR's Georgia Warm Springs Foundation; F. A. Howard; E. M. Clark, Standard Oil of New Jersey; A. P. Sloan, Jr.; D. Brown; J. T. Smith; and W. S. Farish of Standard Oil of New Jersey.

The I.G. Farben files captured at the end of the war confirm the importance of this particular technical transfer for the German Wehrmacht:

> Since the beginning of the war we have been in a position to produce lead tetraethyl solely because, a short time before the outbreak of the war, the Americans had established plants for us ready for production and supplied us with all available experience. In this manner we did not need to perform the difficult work of development because we could start production right away on the basis of all the experience that the Americans had had for years.[13]

In 1938, just before the outbreak of war in Europe, the German Luftwaffe had an urgent requirement for 500 tons of tetraethyl lead. Ethyl was advised by an official of DuPont that such quantities of ethyl would be used by Germany for military purposes.[14] This 500 tons was loaned by the Ethyl Export Corporation of New York to Ethyl G.m.b.H. of Germany, in a transaction arranged by the Reich Air Ministry with I.G. Farben director Mueller-Cunradi. The collateral security was arranged in a letter dated September 21, 1938[15] through Brown Brothers, Harriman & Co. of New York.

Standard Oil of New Jersey and Synthetic Rubber

The transfer of ethyl technology for the Nazi war machine was repeated in the case of synthetic rubber. There is no question that the ability of the German Wehrmacht to fight World War II depended on synthetic rubber—as well as on synthetic petroleum—because Germany has no natural rubber, and war would have been impossible without Farben's synthetic rubber production. Farben had a virtual monopoly of this field and the program to produce the large quantities necessary was financed by the Reich:

> The volume of planned production in this field was far beyond the needs of peacetime economy. The huge costs in-

volved were consistent only with military considerations in which the need for self-sufficiency without regard to cost was decisive.[16]

As in the ethyl technology transfers, Standard Oil of New Jersey was intimately associated with I.G. Farben's synthetic rubber. A series of joint cartel agreements were made in the late 1920s aimed at a joint world monopoly of synthetic rubber. Hitler's Four Year Plan went into effect in 1937 and in 1938 Standard provided I.G. Farben with its new butyl rubber process. On the other hand Standard kept the German buna process secret within the United States and it was not until June 1940 that Firestone and U.S. Rubber were allowed to participate in testing butyl and granted the buna manufacturing licenses. Even then Standard tried to get the U.S. Government to finance a large-scale buna program — reserving its own funds for the more promising butyl process.[17]

Consequently, Standard assistance in Nazi Germany was not limited to oil from coal, although this was the most important transfer. Not only was the process for tetraethyl transferred to I.G. Farben and a plant built in Germany owned jointly by I.G., General Motors, and Standard subsidiaries; but as late as 1939 Standard's German subsidiary designed a German plant for aviation gas. Tetraethyl was shipped on an emergency basis for the Wehrmacht and major assistance was given in production of butyl rubber, while holding secret in the U.S. the Farben process for buna. In other words, Standard Oil of New Jersey (first under president W.C. Teagle and then under W.S. Farish) consistently aided the Nazi war machine while refusing to aid the United States.

This sequence of events was not an accident. President W.S. Farish argued that not to have granted such technical assistance to the Wehrmacht "... would have been unwarranted."[18] The assistance was knowledgeable, ranged over more than a decade, and was so substantive that without it the Wehrmacht could not have gone to war in 1939.

The Deutsche-Amerikanische Petroleum A.G. (DAPAG)

The Standard Oil subsidiary in Germany, Deutsche-Amerikanische Petroleum A.G. (DAPAG), was 94-percent owned by Standard Oil of New Jersey. DAPAG had branches throughout Germany, a refinery at Bremen, and a head office in Hamburg. Through DAPAG, Standard Oil of New Jersey was represented in the inner circles of Naziism—the Keppler Circle and Himmler's Circle of Friends. A director of DAPAG was Karl Linde-mann, also chairman of the International Chamber of Commerce in Ger-many, as well as director of several banks, including the Dresdner Bank, the Deutsche Reichsbank, and the private Nazi-oriented bank of C. Melchior & Company, and numerous corporations including the HAPAG (Hamburg-Amerika Line). Lindemann was a member of Keppler's Circle of Friends as late as 1944 and so gave Standard Oil of New Jersey a representative at the very core of Naziism. Another member of the board of DAPAG was Emil Helffrich, who was an original member of the Keppler Circle.

In sum, Standard Oil of New Jersey had two members of the Keppler Circle as directors of its German wholly owned subsidiary. Payments to the Circle from the Standard Oil subsidiary company, and from Lindemann and Helffrich as individual directors, continued until 1944, the year before the end of World War II.[19]

CHAPTER FIVE

I.T.T. Works Both Sides of the War

> *Thus while I.T.T. Focke-Wolfe planes were bombing Allied ships, and I.T.T. lines were passing information to German submarines, I.T.T. direction finders were saving other ships from torpedoes.* (Anthony Sampson, *The Sovereign State of I.T.T.*, New York: Stein & Day, 1973, p. 40.)

The multi-national giant International Telephone and Telegraph (I.T.T.)[1] was founded in 1920 by Virgin Islands-born entrepreneur Sosthenes Behn. During his lifetime Behn was the epitome of the politicized businessman, earning his profits and building the I.T.T. empire through political maneuverings rather than in the competitive market place. In 1923, through political adroitness, Behn acquired the Spanish telephone monopoly, Compania Telefonica de Espana. In 1924 I.T.T., now backed by the J.P. Morgan firm, bought what later became the International Standard Electric group of manufacturing plants around the world.

The parent board of I.T.T. reflected the J.P. Morgan interests, with Morgan partners Arthur M. Anderson and Russell Leffingwell. The Establishment law firm of Davis, Polk, Wardwell, Gardiner & Reed was represented by the two junior partners, Gardiner & Reed.

DIRECTORS OF I.T.T. IN 1933:

Directors	Affiliation with other Wall Street firms:
Arthur M. ANDERSON	Partner, J.P. MORGAN and New York Trust Company
Hernand BEHN	Bank of America
Sosthenes BEHN	NATIONAL CITY BANK

F. Wilder BELLAMY	Partner in Dominick & Dominick
John W. CUTLER	GRACE NATIONAL BANK, Lee Higginson
George H. GARDINER	Partner in Davis, Polk, Wardwell, Gardiner & Reed
Allen G. HOYT	NATIONAL CITY BANK
Russell C. LEFFINGWELL	Partner J.P. MORGAN and CARNEGIE CORP.
Bradley W. PALMER	Chairman, Executive Committee, UNITED FRUIT
Lansing P. REED	Partner in Davis, Polk, Wardwell, Gardiner & Reed

The National City Bank (NCB) in the Morgan group was represented by two directors, Sosthenes Behn and Allen G. Hoyt. In brief, I.T.T. was a Morgan-controlled company; and we have previously noted the interest of Morgan-controlled companies in war and revolution abroad and political maneuvering in the United States.[2]

In 1930 Behn acquired the German holding company of Standard Elekrizitäts A.G., controlled by I.T.T. (62.0 percent of the voting stock), A.E.G. (31.1 percent of the voting stock) and Felton & Guilleaume (six percent of the voting stock). In this deal Standard acquired two German manufacturing plants and a majority stock interest in Telefonfabrik Berliner A.G. I.T.T. also obtained the Standard subsidiaries in Germany, Ferdinand Schuchardt Berliner Fernsprech-und Telegraphenwerk A.G., as well as Mix & Genest in Berlin, and Suddeutsche Apparate Fabrik G.m.b.H. in Nuremburg.

It is interesting to note in passing that while Sosthenes Behn's I.T.T. controlled telephone companies and manufacturing plants in Germany, the cable traffic between the U.S. and Germany was under the control of Deutsch-Atlantische Telegraphengesellschaft (the German Atlantic Cable Company). This firm, together with the Commercial Cable Company and Western Union Telegraph Company, had a monopoly in transatlantic U.S.-German cable communications. W.A. Harriman & Company took over a block of 625,000 shares in Deutsch-Atlantische in 1925, and the firm's board of directors included an unusual array of characters, many of whom we have met elsewhere. It included, for example, H. F. Albert, the German espionage agent in the United States in World War I; Franklin D. Roosevelt's former business associate von Berenberg-Gossler; and Dr. Cuno, a former German chancellor of the 1923 inflationary era. I.T.T. in the United States was represented on the board by von Guilleaume and Max Warburg of the Warburg banking family.

Baron Kurt von Schröder and the I.T.T.

There is no record that I.T.T. made direct payments to Hitler before the Nazi grab for power in 1933. On the other hand, numerous payments were made to Heinrich Himmler in the late 1930s and in World War II itself through I.T.T. German subsidiaries. The first meeting between Hitler and I.T.T. officials — so far as we know — was reported in August 1933,[3] when Sosthenes Behn and I.T.T. German representative Henry Manne met with Hitler in Berchesgaden. Subsequently, Behn made contact with the Keppler circle (see Chapter Nine) and, through Keppler's influence, Nazi Baron Kurt von Schröder became the guardian of I.T.T. interests in Germany. Schröder acted as the conduit for I.T.T. money funneled to Heinrich Himmler's S.S. organization in 1944, *while World War II was in progress, and the United states was at war with Germany.*[4]

Through Kurt Schröder, Behn and his I.T.T. gained access to the profitable German armaments industry and bought substantial interest in German armaments firms, including Focke-Wolfe aircraft. These armaments operations made handsome profits, which could have been repatriated to the United States parent company. But they were reinvested in German rearmament. This reinvestment of profits in German armament firms suggests that Wall Street claims it was innocent of wrongdoing in German rearmament — and indeed did not even know of Hitler's intentions — are fraudulent. Specifically, I.T.T. purchase of a substantial interest in Focke-Wolfe meant, as Anthony Sampson has pointed out, that I.T.T. was producing German planes used to kill Americans and their allies — and it made excellent profits out of the enterprise.

In Kurt von Schröder, I.T.T. had access to the very heart of the Nazi power elite. Who was Schröder? Baron Kurt von Schröder was born in Hamburg in 1889 into an old, established German banking family. An earlier member of the Schröder family moved to London, changed his name to Schroder (without the dierisis) and organized the banking firm of J. Henry Schroder in London and J. Henry Schroder Banking Corporation in New York. Kurt von Schröder also became a partner in the private Cologne Bankhaus, J. H. Stein & Company, founded in the late eighteenth century. Both Schröder and Stein had been promoters, in company with French financiers, of the 1919 German separatist movement which attempted to split the rich Rhineland away from Germany and its troubles. In this escapade prominent Rhineland industrialists met at J. H. Stein's house on January 7, 1919 and a few months later organized a meeting, with Stein as chairman, to develop public support for the separatist movement. The 1919 action failed. The group tried again in 1923 and spearheaded another movement to break the Rhineland away from Germany to come under the protection of France. This attempt also failed. Kurt von Schröder then linked up with Hitler and the early Nazis, and as in the 1919 and 1923 Rhineland separatist movements, Schröder represented and worked for German industrialists and armaments manufacturers.

In exchange for financial and industrial support arranged by von Schröder, he later gained political prestige. Immediately after the Nazis gained power in 1933 Schröder became the German representative at the Bank for International Settlements, which Quigley calls the apex of the international control system, as well as head of the private bankers group advising the German Reichsbank. Heinrich Himmler appointed Schröder an S.S. Senior Group Leader, and in turn Himmler became a prominent member of Keppler's Circle. (See Chapter Nine.)

In 1938 the Schroder Bank in London became the German financial agent in Great Britain, represented at financial meetings by its Managing Director (and a director of the Bank of England), F.C. Tiarks. By World War II Baron Schröder had in this manner acquired an impressive list of political and banking connections reflecting a widespread influence; it was even reported to the U.S. Kilgore Committee that Schröder was influential enough in 1940 to bring Pierre Laval to power in France. As listed by the Kilgore Committee, Schröder's political acquisitions in the early 1940s were as follows:

SS Senior Group Leader.
Iron Cross of First and Second Class.
Swedish Consul General.
International Chamber of Commerce - Member of administrative committee.
Council of Reich Post Office - Member of advisory board.
German Industrial and Commerce Assembly - Presiding member.
Reich Board of Economic Affairs - Member.
Deutsche Reichsbahn - President of administrative board.

Trade Group for Wholesale and Foreign Trade - Manager.
Akademie für Deutsches Recht (Academy of Germany Law) - Member.
City of Cologne - Councilor.
University of Cologne - Member of board of trustees.
Kaiser Wilhelm Foundation - Senator.
Advisory Council of German-Albanians.
Goods Clearing Bureau - Member.
Working Committee of Reich Group for Industry and Commerce - Deputy chairman.[5]

Schröder's banking connections were equally impressive and his business connections (not listed here) would take up two pages:

Bank for International Settlements - Member of the directorate.

J.H. Stein & Co, Cologne - Partner (Banque Worms was French correspondent).

Deutsche Reichsbank, Berlin. Adviser to board of directors.

Wirtschaftsgruppe Private Bankegewerbe - Leader.

Deutsche Verkehrs-Kredit-Bank, A.G., Berlin (Controlled by Deutsche Reichsbank) - Chairman of board of directors.

Deutsche Ueberseeische Bank (Controlled by Deutsche Bank, Berlin) - Director.[6]

This was the Schröder who, after 1933, represented Sosthenes Behn of I.T.T. and I.T.T. interests in Nazi Germany. Precisely because Schröder had these excellent political connections with Hitler and the Nazi State, Behn appointed Schröder to the boards of all the I.T.T. German companies: Standard Electrizitatswerke A.G. in Berlin, C. Lorenz A.G. of Berlin, and Mix & Genest A.G. (in which Standard had a 94-percent participation).

In the mid-1930s another link was forged between Wall Street and Schröder, this time through the Rockefellers. In 1936 the underwriting and general securities business handled by J. Henry Schroder Banking Corporation in New York was merged into a new investment banking firm — Schroder, Rockefeller & Company, Inc. at 48 Wall Street. Carlton P. Fuller of Schroder Banking Corporation became president and Avery Rockefeller, son of Percy Rockefeller (brother of John D. Rockefeller) became vice president and director of the new firm. Previously, Avery Rockefeller had been associated behind the scenes with J. Henry Schroder Banking Corporation; the new firm brought him out into the open.[7]

Westrick, Texaco, and I.T.T.

I.T.T. had yet another conduit to Nazi Germany, through German attorney Dr. Gerhard Westrick. Westrick was one of a select group of Germans who had conducted espionage in the United States during World War I. The group included not only Kurt von Schröder and Westrick but also Franz von Papen — whom we shall meet in company with James Paul Warburg of the Bank of Manhattan in Chapter Ten — and Dr. Heinrich Albert. Albert, supposedly German commercial attaché in the U.S. in

World War I, was actually in charge of financing von Papen's espionage program. After World War I Westrick and Albert formed the law firm of Albert & Westrick which specialized in, and profited heavily from, the Wall Street reparations loans. The Albert & Westrick firm handled the German end of the J. Henry Schroder Banking loans, while the John Foster Dulles firm of Sullivan and Cromwell in New York handled the U.S. end of the Schroder loans.

Just prior to World War II the Albert-Papen-Westrick espionage operation in the United States began to repeat itself, only this time around the American authorities were more alert. Westrick came to the U.S. in 1940, supposedly as a commercial attaché but in fact as Ribbentrop's personal representative. A stream of visitors to the influential Westrick included prominent directors of U.S. petroleum and industrial firms, and this brought Westrick to the attention of the FBI.

Westrick at this time became a director of all I.T.T. operations in Germany, in order to protect I.T.T. interests during the expected U.S. involvement in the European war.[8] Among his other enterprises Westrick attempted to persuade Henry Ford to cut off supplies to Britain, and the favored treatment given by the Nazis to Ford interests in France suggests that Westrick was partially successful in neutralizing U.S. aid to Britain.

Although Westrick's most important wartime business connection in the United States was with International Telephone and Telegraph, he also represented other U.S. firms, including Underwood Elliott Fisher, owner of the German company Mercedes Buromaschinen A.G.; Eastman Kodak, which had a Kodak subsidiary in Germany; and the International Milk Corporation, with a Hamburg subsidiary. Among Westrick's deals (and the one which received the most publicity) was a contract for Texaco to supply oil to the German Navy, which he arranged with Torkild Rieber, chairman of the board of Texaco Company.

In 1940 Rieber discussed an oil deal with Hermann Goering, and Westrick in the United States worked for Texas Oil Company. His automobile was bought with Texaco funds, and Westrick's driver's license application gave Texaco as his business address. These activities were publicized on August 12, 1940. Rieber subsequently resigned from Texaco and Westrick returned to Germany. Two years later Rieber was chairman of South Carolina Shipbuilding and Dry Docks, supervising construction of more than $10 million of U.S. Navy ships, and a director of the Guggenheim family's Barber Asphalt Corporation and Seaboard Oil Company of Ohio.[9]

I.T.T. in Wartime Germany

In 1939 I.T.T. in the United States controlled Standard Elektrizitäts in Germany, and in turn Standard Elektrizitäts controlled 94 percent of Mix & Genest. On the board of Standard Elektrizitäts was Baron Kurt von Schröder, a Nazi banker at the core of Naziism, and Emil Heinrich Meyer, brother-in-law of Secretary of State Keppler (founder of the Keppler Circle) and a director of German General Electric. Schröder and Meyer were also directors of Mix & Genest and the other I.T.T. subsidiary, C. Lorenz Company; both of these I.T.T. subsidiaries were monetary contributors to Himmler's Circle of Friends — *i.e.*, the Nazi S.S. slush fund. As late as 1944, Mix & Genest contributed 5,000 RM to Himmler and Lorenz contributed 20,000 RM. In short, during World War II International Telephone and Telegraph was making cash payments to S.S. leader Heinrich Himmler.[10] These payments enabled I.T.T. to protect its investment in Focke-Wolfe, an aircraft manufacturing firm producing fighter aircraft used against the United States.

The interrogation of Kurt von Schröder on November 19, 1945 points up the deliberate nature of the close and profitable relationship between Colonel Sosthenes Behn of I.T.T., Westrick, Schröder, and the Nazi war machine during World War II, and that *this was a deliberate and knowledgeable relationship*:

Q. You have [told] us in your earlier testimony, a number of companies in Germany in which the International Telephone and Telegraph Company or the Standard Electric Company had a participation. Did either International Telephone and Telegraph Company or the Standard Electric Company have a participation in any other company in Germany?

A. Yes. The Lorenz Company, shortly before the war, took a participation of about 25 percent in Focke-Wolfe A.G. in Bremen. Focke-Wolfe was making airplanes for the German Air Ministry. I believe that later as Focke-Wolfe expanded and took in more capital that the interest of Lorenz Company dropped a little below this 25 percent.

Q. So this participation in Focke-Wolfe by Lorenz Company began after Lorenz Company was nearly 100-percent owned and controlled by Colonel Behn through the International Telephone and Telegraph Company?

A. Yes.

Q. Did Colonel Behen [*sic*] approve of this investment by the Lorenz Company in Focke-Wolfe?

A. I am confident that Colonel Behn approved before his representatives who were in close touch with him formally approved the transaction.

Q. What year was it that the Lorenz Company made the investment which gave it this 25 percent participation in Focke-Wolfe?

A. I remember it was shortly before the outbreak of war, that is, shortly before the invasion of Poland. [Ed: 1939]

Q. Would Westrick know all about the details of the participations of Lorenz Company in Focke-Wolfe, A.G. of Bremen?

A. Yes. Better than I would.

Q. What was the size of the investment that Lorenz Company made in the Focke-Wolfe A.G., of Bremen, which gave them the initial 25 percent participation?

A. 250,000 thousand RM initially, and this was substantially increased, but I don't recall the extent of the additional investments that Lorenz Company made to this Focke-Wolfe A.G. of Bremen.

Q. From 1933, until the outbreak of the European War, was Colonel Behn in a position to transfer the profits from investments of his companies in Germany to his companies in the United States?

A. Yes. While it would have required that his companies take a little less than the full dividends because of the difficulty of securing foreign exchange, the great bulk of the profits could have been transferred to the company of Colonel Behn in the United States. However, Colonel Behn did not elect to do this and at no time did he ask me if I could accomplish this for him. Instead, he appeared to be perfectly content to have all the profits of the companies in Germany, which he and his interests controlled, reinvesting these profits in new buildings and machinery and any other enterprises engaged in producing armaments.

Another one of these enterprises, Huth and Company, G.m.b.H., of Berlin, which made radio and radar parts, many of which were used in equipment going to the German Armed Forces. The Lorenz Company as I recall it [had] a 50-percent participation in Huth and Company. The Lorenz Company also had a small subsidiary which acted as a sales agency for the Lorenz Company to private customers.

Q. You were a member of the board of Lorenz Company's board of director, from about 1935 up to the present time. During this time, Lorenz Company and some of the other companies, such as Focke-Wolfe with which it had large participations, were engaged in the manufacture of equipment for armaments and war production. Did you know or did you hear of any protest made by Colonel Behn or his representatives against these companies engaged in these activities preparing Germany for war?

A. No.

Q. Are you positive that there was no other occasion in which you were asked by either Westrick, Mann [sic], Colonel Behn or any other person connected with the International Telephone and Telegraphic Company interests in Germany, to intervene on behalf of the company with the German authorities.

A. Yes. I don't remember any request for my intervention in any matter of importance to the Lorenz Company or any other International Telephone and Telegraph interests in Germany.

I have read the record of this interrogation and I swear that the answers I have given to the question of Messrs. Adams and Pajus are true to the best of knowledge and belief. s/Kurt von Schröder

It was this story of I.T.T.-Nazi cooperation during World War II and I.T.T. association with Nazi Kurt von Schröder that I.T.T. *wanted* to conceal — and almost was successful in concealing. James Stewart Martin recounts how during the planning meetings of the Finance Division of the Control Commission he was assigned to work with Captain Norbert A. Bogdan, who out of uniform was vice president of the J. Henry Schroder Banking Corporation of New York. Martin relates that "Captain Bogdan had argued vigorously against investigation of the Stein Bank on the grounds that it was 'small potatoes.' "[11] Shortly after blocking this maneuver, two permanent members of Bogdan's staff applied for permission to investigate the Stein Bank — although Cologne had not yet fallen to U.S. forces. Martin recalls that "The Intelligence Division blocked that one," and so some information on the Stein-Schröder Bank-I.T.T. operation survived.

PART TWO

WALL STREET AND
FUNDS FOR HITLER

CHAPTER SIX

Henry Ford and the Nazis

I would like to outline the importance attached by high [Nazi] officials to respect the desire and maintain the good will of "Ford," and by "Ford" I mean your father, yourself, and the Ford Motor Company, Dearborn. (Josiah E. Dubois, Jr., *Generals in Grey Suits,* London: The Bodley Head, 1953, p. 250.)

Henry Ford is often seen to be something of an enigma among the Wall Street elite. For many years in the 20s and 30s Ford was popularly known as an enemy of the financial establishment. Ford accused Morgan and others of using war and revolution as a road to profit and their influence in social systems as a means of personal advancement. By 1938 Henry Ford, in his public statements, had divided financiers into two classes: those who profited from war and used their influence to bring about war for profit, and the "constructive" financiers. Among the latter group he now included the House of Morgan. During a 1938 *New York Times* interview[1] Ford averred that:

Somebody once said that sixty families have directed the destinies of the nation. It might well be said that if somebody would focus the spotlight on twenty-five persons who handle the nation's finances, the world's real warmakers would be brought into bold relief.

The *Times* reporter asked Ford how he equated this assessment with his long-standing criticism of the House of Morgan, to which Ford replied:

There is a constructive and a destructive Wall Street. The House of Morgan represents the constructive. I have known Mr. Morgan for many years. He backed and supported Thomas Edison, who was also my good friend . . . .

After expounding on the evils of limited agricultural production — allegedly brought about by Wall Street — Ford continued,

> . . . *if these financiers had their way we'd be in a war now. They want war because they make money out of such conflict — out of the human misery that wars bring.*

On the other hand, when we probe behind these public statements we find that Henry Ford and son Edsel Ford have been in the forefront of American businessmen who try to walk both sides of every ideological fence in search of profit. Using Ford's own criteria, the Fords are among the "destructive" elements.

It was Henry Ford who in the 1930s built the Soviet Union's first modern automobile plant (located at Gorki) and which in the 50s and 60s produced the trucks used by the North Vietnamese to carry weapons and munitions for use against Americans.[2] At about the same time, Henry Ford was also the most famous of Hitler's foreign backers, and he was rewarded in the 1930s for this long-lasting support with the highest Nazi decoration for foreigners.

This Nazi favor aroused a storm of controversy in the United States and ultimately degenerated into an exchange of diplomatic notes between the German Government and the State Department. While Ford publically protested that he did not like totalitarian governments, we find in practice that Ford knowingly profited from both sides of World War II — from French and German plants producing vehicles at a profit for the Wehrmacht, and from U.S. plants building vehicles at a profit for the U.S. Army.

Henry Ford's protestations of innocence suggest, as we shall see in this chapter, that he did not approve of Jewish financiers profiting from war (as some have), but if anti-Semitic Morgan[3] and Ford profited from war that was acceptable, moral and "constructive."

Henry Ford: Hitler's First Foreign Backer

On December 20, 1922 the *New York Times* reported[4] that automobile manufacturer Henry Ford was financing Adolph Hitler's nationalist and anti-Semitic movements in Munich. Simultaneously, the Berlin newspaper *Berliner Tageblatt* appealed to the American Ambassador in Berlin to investigate and halt Henry Ford's intervention into German domestic affairs. It was reported that Hitler's foreign backers had

New York Times, August 1, 1938

HITLER ACCLAIMED BY 200,000 IN FETE

Wild Scenes of Enthusiasm Mark Parade of Athletes at the Breslau Festival

SUDETENS BREAK RANKS

40,000 Swarm Around Stand of Chancellor and Girls Give Flowers in Homage

Wireless to THE NEW YORK TIMES.

BRESLAU, Germany, July 31.— The German National Gymnastic Festival, which in the last week has drawn to Breslau German-speaking persons from all parts of the world, reached a climax today when 200,- 000 participants, 40,000 of them from the Sudeten region of Czechoslovakia, marched past Chancellor Hitler and proclaimed their constancy to their "racial" origin.

The last previous festival of this kind was at Stuttgart in 1933, when the extension of the German State frontiers to the German State confines was still far from attainment. Today this end is in part realized, and its further realization is a burning issue.

Seldom has such a storm of adulation broken around the enigmatic figure of Hitler as occurred this morning on the Schlossplatz here.

HENRY FORD GETTING HIGH HONOR FROM GERMAN GOVERNMENT

The industrialist receiving the Grand Cross of the German Eagle, a decoration for distinguished foreigners, on the occasion of his seventy-fifth birthday. The presentation marked the first time that the award has been made in this country. At the left is Fritz Heiler, German consular representative at Detroit, and at the right Karl Kapp, German consul at Cleveland.

Associated Press

New York Times, December 20, 1922

BERLIN HEARS FORD IS BACKING HITLER

Bavarian Anti-Semitic Chief Has American's Portrait and Book in His Office,

SPENDS MONEY LAVISHLY

One German Paper Appeals to the United States Ambassador to Make Investigation.

Copyright, 1922, by The New York Times Company.
Special Cable to THE NEW YORK TIMES.

BERLIN, Dec. 19.—A rumor is current here that Henry Ford, the American automobile manufacturer, is financing Adolph Hitler's nationalist and anti-Semitic movement in Munich. Indeed, the Berlin Tageblatt has made an appeal to the American Ambassador in Berlin to investigate and interfere.

Doubtless there is some ground for suspicion that Hitler is spending foreign money, for the paper marks his admirers throughout Germany would tribute toward his movement. His personal and business... hardly suffice to pay for such large

ANTI-SEMITIC RIOTS SPREAD IN RUMANIA

Parade of Jews Broken Up by Students at Jassy and Many Are Beaten.

BUCHAREST, Rumania, Dec. 19 (Jewish Telegraphic Agency).—A large number of Jews at Jassy were severely beaten and three of them were wounded when a mob of students attacked a demonstration yesterday which was arranged by Jews as a protest against attacks on Jews throughout the country.

The object of the parade was to point out the need for Government protection of the Jews, who, the leaders declare, have been made the object of nationwide aggression in order to bring about repeal of the constitutional clauses guaranteeing their complete enfranchisement.

Daily demonstrations against Jews continue in the capital at Klausenberg, attacks at Czernowitz and Klausenberg, according to reports from these places, the demonstrations often ending in street fights with the police in their efforts to disperse the mob.

The offices of liberal newspapers which protested against the anti-Jewish aggression are being guarded by police and the street patrols have been reinforced.

SUNDAY FOR WORLD PEACE.

Federal Council Asks 100,000 Churches to Observe Day.

WASHINGTON, Dec. 19.—The Federal Council of Churches of Christ in America issued today a request to 100,000 congregations in the United States to observe Dec. 28 as "World Peace Sunday"...

furnished a "spacious headquarters" with a "host of highly paid lieutenants and officials." Henry Ford's portrait was prominently displayed on the walls of Hitler's personal office:

> The wall behind his desk in Hitler's private office is decorated with a large picture of Henry Ford. In the antechamber there is a large table covered with books, nearly all of which are a translation of a book written and published by Henry Ford.[5]

The same *New York Times* report commented that the previous Sunday Hitler had reviewed,

> The so-called Storming Battalion . . . 1,000 young men in brand new uniforms and armed with revolvers and blackjacks, while Hitler and his henchmen drove around in two powerful brand-new autos.

The *Times* made a clear distinction between the German monarchist parties and Hitler's anti-Semitic fascist party. Henry Ford, it was noted, ignored the Hohenzollern monarchists and put his money into the Hitlerite revolutionary movement.

These Ford funds were used by Hitler to foment the Bavarian rebellion. The rebellion failed, and Hitler was captured and subsequently brought to trial. In February 1923 at the trial, vice president Auer of the Bavarian Diet testified:

> The Bavarian Diet has long had the information that the Hitler movement was partly financed by an American anti-Semitic chief, who is Henry Ford. Mr. Ford's interest in the Bavarian anti-Semitic movement began a year ago when one of Mr. Ford's agents, seeking to sell tractors, came in contact with Diedrich Eichart, the notorious Pan-German. Shortly after, Herr Eichart asked Mr. Ford's agent for financial aid. The agent returned to America and immediately Mr. Ford's money began coming to Munich.
>
> Herr Hitler openly boasts of Mr. Ford's support and praises Mr. Ford as a great individualist and a great anti-Semite. A photograph of Mr. Ford hangs in Herr Hitler's quarters, which is the center of monarchist movement.[6]

Hitler received a mild and comfortable prison sentence for his Bavarian revolutionary activities. The rest from more active pursuits enabled him to write *Mein Kampf*. Henry Ford's book, *The International Jew*, earlier circulated by the Nazis, was translated by them into a dozen languages, and Hitler utilized sections of the book verbatim in writing *Mein Kampf*.[1]

We shall see later that Hitler's backing in the late 20s and early 30s came from the chemical, steel, and electrical industry cartels, rather than directly from individual industrialists. In 1928 Henry Ford merged his German assets with those of the I.G. Farben chemical cartel. A substantial holding, 40 percent of Ford Motor A.G. of Germany, was transferred to I.G. Farben; Carl Bosch of I.G. Farben became head of Ford A.G. Motor in Germany. Simultaneously, in the United States Edsel Ford joined the board of American I.G. Farben. (See Chapter Two.)

Henry Ford Receives a Nazi Medal

A decade later, in August 1938 — after Hitler had achieved power with the aid of the cartels — Henry Ford received the Grand Cross of the German Eagle, a Nazi decoration for distinguished foreigners. The *New York Times* reported it was the first time the Grand Cross had been awarded in the United States and was to celebrate Henry Ford's 75th birthday.[8]

The decoration raised a storm of criticism within Zionist circles in the U.S. Ford backed off to the extent of publicly meeting with Rabbi Leo Franklin of Detroit to express his sympathy for the plight of German Jews:

> *My acceptance of a medal from the German people [said Ford] does not, as some people seem to think, involve any sympathy on my part with naziism. Those who have known me for many years realize that anything that breeds hate is repulsive to me.*[9]

The Nazi medal issue was picked up in a Cleveland speech by Secretary of Interior Harold Ickes. Ickes criticized both Henry Ford and Colonel Charles A. Lindbergh for accepting Nazi medals. The curious part of the Ickes speech, made at a Cleveland Zionist Society banquet, was his criticism of "wealthy Jews" and *their* acquisition and use of wealth:

> *A mistake made by a non-Jewish millionaire reflects upon him alone, but a false step made by a Jewish man of wealth reflects upon his whole race. This is harsh and unjust, but it is a fact that must be faced.*[10]

Perhaps Ickes was tangentially referring to the roles of the Warburgs in the I.G. Farben cartel: Warburgs were on the board of I.G. Farben in the U.S. and Germany. In 1938 the Warburgs were being ejected by the Nazis from Germany. Other German Jews, such as the Oppenheim bankers, made their peace with the Nazis and were granted "honorary Aryan status."

Ford Motor Company Assists the German War Effort

A post-war Congressional subcommittee investigating American support for the Nazi military effort described the manner in which the Nazis succeeded in obtaining U.S. technical and financial assistance as "quite fantastic."[11] Among other evidence the Committee was shown a memorandum prepared in the offices of Ford-Werke A.G. on November 25, 1941, written by Dr. H. F. Albert to R. H. Schmidt, then president of the board of Ford-Werke A.G. The memo cited the advantages of having a majority of the German firm held by Ford Motor Company in Detroit. German Ford had been able to exchange Ford parts for rubber and critical war materials needed in 1938 and 1939 "and they would not have been able to do that if Ford had not been owned by the United States." Further, with a majority American interest German Ford would "more easily be able to step in and dominate the Ford holdings throughout Europe." It was even reported to the Committee that two top German Ford officials had been in a bitter personal feud about who was to control Ford of England, such "that one of them finally got up and left the room in disgust."

According to evidence presented to the Committee, Ford-Werke A.G. was technically transformed in the late 1930s into a German company. All vehicles and their parts were produced in Germany, by German workers using German materials under German direction and exported to European and overseas territories of the United States and Great Britain. Any needed foreign raw materials, rubber and nonferrous metals, were obtained through the American Ford Company. American influence had been more or less converted into a supporting position (*Hilfsstellung*) for the German Ford plants.

At the outbreak of the war Ford-Werke placed itself at the disposal of the Wehrmacht for armament production. It was assumed by the Nazis that as long as Ford-Werke A.G. had an American majority, it would be possible to bring the remaining European Ford companies under German influence — *i.e.*, that of Ford-Werke A.G. — and so execute Nazi

"Greater European" policies in the Ford plants in Amsterdam, Antwerp, Paris, Budapest, Bucharest, and Copenhagen:

> *A majority, even if only a small one, of Americans is essential for the transmittal of the newest American models, as well as American production and sales methods. With the abolition of the American majority, this advantage, as well as the intervention of the Ford Motor Company to obtain raw materials and exports, would be lost, and the German plant would practically only be worth its machine capacity.*[12]

And, of course, this kind of strict neutrality, taking an international rather than a national viewpoint, had earlier paid off for Ford Motor Company in the Soviet Union, where Ford was held in high regard as the ultimate of technical and economic efficiency to be achieved by the Stakhanovites.

In July 1942 word filtered back to Washington from Ford of France about Ford's activities on behalf of the German war effort in Europe. The incriminating information was promptly buried and even today only part of the known documentation can be traced in Washington.

We do know, however, that the U.S. Consul General in Algeria had possession of a letter from Maurice Dollfuss of French Ford — who claimed to be the first Frenchman to go to Berlin after the fall of France — to Edsel Ford about a plan by which Ford Motor could contribute to the Nazi war effort. French Ford was able to produce 20 trucks a day for the Wehrmacht, which [wrote Dollfuss] is better than,

> *. . . our less fortunate French competitors are doing. The reason is that our trucks are in very large demand by the German authorities and I believe that as long as the war goes on and at least for some period of time, all that we shall produce will be taken by the German authorities. . . . I will satisfy myself by telling you that . . . the attitude you have taken, together with your father, of strict neutrality, has been an invaluable asset for the production of your companies in Europe.*[13]

Dollfuss disclosed that profits from this German business were already 1.6 million francs, and net profits for 1941 were no less than 58,000,-000 francs — because the Germans paid promptly for Ford's output. On receipt of this news Edsel Ford cabled:

> *Delighted to hear you are making progress. Your letters*
> *most interesting. Fully realize great handicap you are working*
> *under. Hope you and family well. Regards.*
>
> *s/Edsel Ford*[14]

Although there is evidence that European plants owned by Wall Street interests were not bombed by the U.S. Air Force in World War II, this restriction apparently did not reach the British Bombing Command. In March 1942 the Royal Air Force bombed the Ford plant at Poissy, France. A subsequent letter from Edsel Ford to Ford General Manager Sorenson about this RAF raid commented, "Photographs of the plant on fire were published in American newspapers but fortunately no reference was made to the Ford Motor Company."[15] In any event, the Vichy government paid Ford Motor Company 38 million francs as compensation for damage done to the Poissy plant. This was not reported in the U.S. press and would hardly be appreciated by those Americans at war with Naziism. Dubois asserts that these *private* messages from Ford in Europe were passed to Edsel Ford by Assistant Secretary of State Breckenridge Long. This was the same Secretary Long who one year later suppressed *private* messages through the State Department concerning the extermination of Jews in Europe.[16] Disclosure of those messages conceivably could have been used to assist those desperate people.

A U.S. Air Force bombing intelligence report written in 1943 noted that,

> *Principal wartime activities [of the Ford plant] are proba-*
> *bly manufacture of light trucks and of spare parts for all the Ford*
> *trucks and cars in service in Axis Europe (including captured*
> *Russian Molotovs).*[16]

The Russian Molotovs were of course manufactured by the Ford-built works at Gorki, Russia. In France during the war, passenger automobile production was entirely replaced by military vehicles and for this purpose three large additional buildings were added to the Poissy factory. The main building contained about 500 machine tools, "all imported from the United States and including a fair sprinkling of the more complex types, such as Gleason gear cutters, Bullard automatics and Ingersoll borers."[17]

Ford also extended its wartime activities into North Africa. In December 1941 a new Ford Company, Ford-Afrique, was registered in France and granted all the rights of the former Ford Motor Company, Ltd.

of England in Algeria, Tunisia, French Morocco, French Equatorial, and French West Africa. North Africa was not accessible to British Ford so this new Ford Company — registered in German-occupied France — was organized to fill the gap. The directors were pro-Nazi and included Maurice Dollfuss (Edsel Ford's correspondent) and Roger Messis (described by the U.S. Algiers Consul General as "known to this office by repute as unscrupulous, is stated to be a 100 percent pro-German").[18]

The U.S. Consul General also reported that propaganda was common in Algiers about

> . . . *the collaboration of French-German-American capital and the questionable sincerity of the American war effort, [there] is already pointing an accusing finger at a transaction which has been for long a subject of discussion in commercial circles.*[19]

In brief, there is documentary evidence that Ford Motor Company worked on both sides of World War II. If the Nazi industrialists brought to trial at Nuremburg were guilty of crimes against mankind, then so must be their fellow collaborators in the Ford family, Henry and Edsel Ford. However, the Ford story was concealed by Washington — apparently like almost everything else that could touch upon the name and sustenance of the Wall Street financial elite.

CHAPTER SEVEN

Who Financed Adolf Hitler?

The funding of Hitler and the Nazi movement has yet to be explored in exhaustive depth. The only published examination of Hitler's personal finances is an article by Oron James Hale, "Adolph Hitler: Taxpayer,"[1] which records Adolph's brushes with the German tax authorities before he became *Reichskanzler*. In the 1920s Hitler presented himself to the German tax man as merely an impoverished writer living on bank loans, with an automobile bought on credit. Unfortunately, the original records used by Hale do not yield the source of Hitler's income, loans, or credit, and German law "did not require self-employed or professional persons to disclose in detail the sources of income or the nature of services rendered."[2] Obviously the funds for the automobiles, private secretary Rudolf Hess, another assistant, a chauffeur, and expenses incurred by political activity, came from somewhere. But, like Leon Trotsky's 1917 stay in New York, it is hard to reconcile Hitler's known expenditures with the precise source of his income.

Some Early Hitler Backers

We do know that prominent European and American industrialists were sponsoring all manner of totalitarian political groups at that time, including Communists and various Nazi groups. The U.S Kilgore Committee records that:

> By 1919 Krupp was already giving financial aid to one of the reactionary political groups which sowed the seed of the present Nazi ideology. Hugo Stinnes was an early contributor to the Nazi Party (National Socialistische Deutsche Arbeiter Partei). By 1924 other prominent industrialists and financiers, among them Fritz Thyssen, Albert Voegler, Adolph [sic] Kirdorf, and Kurt von Schröder, were secretly giving substantial sums to the Nazis. In 1931 members of the coalowners' association which Kirdorf

headed pledged themselves to pay 50 pfennigs for each ton of coal sold, the money to go to the organization which Hitler was building.[3]

Hitler's 1924 Munich trial yielded evidence that the Nazi Party received $20,000 from Nuremburg industrialists. The most interesting name from this period is that of Emil Kirdorf, who had earlier acted as conduit for financing German involvement in the Bolshevik Revolution.[4] Kirdorf's role in financing Hitler was, in his own words:

> *In 1923 I came into contact for the first time with the National-Socialist movement. . . . I first heard the Fuehrer in the Essen Exhibition Hall. His clear exposition completely convinced and overwhelmed me. In 1927 I first met the Fuehrer personally. I travelled to Munich and there had a conversation with the Fuehrer in the Bruckmann home. During four and a half hours Adolf Hitler explained to me his programme in detail. I then begged the Fuehrer to put together the lecture he had given me in the form of a pamphlet. I then distributed this pamphlet in my name in business and manufacturing circles.*
>
> *Since then I have placed myself completely at the disposition of his movement. Shortly after our Munich conversation, and as a result of the pamphlet which the Fuehrer composed and I distributed, a number of meetings took place between the Fuehrer and leading personalities in the field of industry. For the last time before the taking over of power, the leaders of industry met in my house together with Adolf Hitler, Rudolf Hess, Hermann Goering and other leading personalities of the party.*[5]

In 1925 the Hugo Stinnes family contributed funds to convert the Nazi weekly *Volkischer Beobachter* to a daily publication. Putzi Hanfstaengl, Franklin D. Roosevelt's friend and protegé, provided the remaining funds.[6] Table 7-1 summarizes presently known financial contributions and the business associations of contributors from the United States. Putzi is not listed in Table 7-1 as he was neither industrialist nor financier.

In the early 1930s financial assistance to Hitler began to flow more readily. There took place in Germany a series of meetings, irrefutably documented in several sources, between German industrialists, Hitler himself, and more often Hitler's representatives Hjalmar Schacht and

Rudolf Hess. The critical point is that the German industrialists financing Hitler were predominantly directors of cartels with American associations, ownership, participation, or some form of subsidiary connection. The Hitler backers were not, by and large, firms of purely German origin, or representative of German family business. Except for Thyssen and Kirdorf, in most cases they were the German multi-national firms — *i.e.*,I.G. Farben, A.E.G., DAPAG, *etc.* These multi-nationals had been built up by American loans in the 1920s, and in the early 1930s had American directors and heavy American financial participation.

One flow of foreign political funds not considered here is that reported from the European-based Royal Dutch Shell, Standard Oil's great competitor in the 20s and 30s, and the giant brainchild of Anglo-Dutch businessman Sir Henri Deterding. It has been widely asserted that Henri Deterding personally financed Hitler. This argument is made, for instance, by biographer Glyn Roberts in *The Most Powerful Man in the World*. Roberts notes that Deterding was impressed with Hitler as early as 1921:

> . . . *and the Dutch press reported that, through the agent Georg Bell, he [Deterding] had placed at Hitler's disposal, while the party was "still in long clothes," no less than four million guilders.*[7]

It was reported (by Roberts) that in 1931 Georg Bell, Deterding's agent, attended meetings of Ukrainian Patriots in Paris "as joint delegate of Hitler and Deterding."[8] Roberts also reports:

> *Deterding was accused, as Edgar Ansell Mowrer testifies in his* Germany Puts the Clock Back, *of putting up a large sum of money for the Nazis on the understanding that success would give him a more favored position in the German oil market. On other occasions, figures as high as £55,000,000 were mentioned.*[9]

Biographer Roberts really found Deterding's strong anti-Bolshevism distasteful, and rather than present hard evidence of funding he is inclined to assume rather than prove that Deterding was pro-Hitler. But pro-Hitlerism is not a necessary consequence of anti-Bolshevism; in any event Roberts offers no proof of finance, and hard evidence of Deterding's involvement was not found by this author.

Mowrer's book contains neither index nor footnotes as to the source of his information and Roberts has no specific evidence for his accusations. There is circumstantial evidence that Deterding was pro-Nazi. He later went to live in Hitler's Germany and increased his share of the German petroleum market. So there may have been some contributions, but these have not been proven.

Similarly, in France (on January 11, 1932), Paul Fauré, a member of the *Chambre des Députés*, accused the French industrial firm of Schneider-Creuzot of financing Hitler — and incidentally implicated Wall Street in other financing channels.[10]

The Schneider group is a famous firm of French armaments manufacturers. After recalling the Schneider influence in establishment of Fascism in Hungary and its extensive international armaments operations, Paul Fauré turns to Hitler, and quotes from the French paper *Le Journal*, "that Hitler had received 300,000 Swiss gold francs" from subscriptions opened in Holland under the case of a university professor named von Bissing. The Skoda plant at Pilsen, stated Paul Fauré, was controlled by the French Schneider family, and it was the Skoda directors von Duschnitz and von Arthaber who made the subscriptions to Hitler. Fauré concluded:

> . . . I am disturbed to see the directors of Skoda, controlled by Schneider, subsidizing the electoral campaign of M. Hitler; I am disturbed to see your firms, your financiers, your industrial cartels unite themselves with the most nationalistic of Germans . . . .

Again, no hard evidence was found for this alleged flow of Hitler funds.

Fritz Thyssen and W.A. Harriman Company of New York

Another elusive case of reported financing of Hitler is that of Fritz Thyssen, the German steel magnate who associated himself with the Nazi movement in the early 20s. When interrogated in 1945 under Project Dustbin,[11] Thyssen recalled that he was approached in 1923 by General Ludendorf at the time of French evacuation of the Ruhr. Shortly after this meeting Thyssen was introduced to Hitler and provided funds for the Nazis through General Ludendorf. In 1930-1931 Emil Kirdorf approached Thyssen and subsequently sent Rudolf Hess to negotiate further funding for the Nazi Party. This time Thyssen arranged a credit of 250,000 marks at the Bank Voor Handel en Scheepvaart N.V. at 18 Zuidblaak in Rotterdam, Holland, founded in 1918 with H. J. Kouwenhoven and D. C. Schutte as managing partners.[12] This bank was a subsidiary of the August Thyssen Bank of Germany (formerly von der Heydt's Bank A.G.). It was Thyssen's personal banking operation, and it was affiliated with the W. A. Harriman financial interests in New York. Thyssen reported to his Project Dustbin interrogators that:

> *I chose a Dutch bank because I did not want to be mixed up with German banks in my position, and because I thought it was better to do business with a Dutch bank, and I thought I would have the Nazis a little more in my hands.*[13]

Thyssen's book *I Paid Hitler*, published in 1941, was purported to be written by Fritz Thyssen himself, although Thyssen denies authorship. The book claims that funds for Hitler — about one million marks — came mainly from Thyssen himself. *I Paid Hitler* has other unsupported assertions, for example that Hitler was actually descended from an illegitimate child of the Rothschild family. Supposedly Hitler's grandmother, Frau Schickelgruber, had been a servant in the Rothschild household and while there became pregnant:

> ... *an inquiry once ordered by the late Austrian chancellor, Engelbert Dollfuss, yielded some interesting results, owing to the fact that the dossiers of the police department of the Austro-Hungarian monarch were remarkably complete.*[14]

This assertion concerning Hitler's illegitimacy is refuted entirely in a more solidly based book by Eugene Davidson, which implicates the Frankenberger family, not the Rothschild family.

In any event, and more relevant from our viewpoint, the August Thyssen front bank in Holland — *i.e.*, the Bank voor Handel en Scheepvaart N.V. — controlled the Union Banking Corporation in New York. The Harrimans had a financial interest in, and E. Roland Harriman (Averell's brother) was a director of, this Union Banking Corporation. The Union Banking Corporation of New York City was a joint Thyssen-Harriman operation with the following directors in 1932:[15]

E. Roland HARRIMAN	Vice president of W. A. Harriman & Co., New York
H. J. KOUWENHOVEN	Nazi banker, managing partner of August Thyssen Bank and Bank voor Handel Scheepvaart N.V. (the transfer bank for Thyssen's funds)

TABLE 7-1: FINANCIAL LINKS BETWEEN U.S. INDUSTRIALISTS AND ADOLF HITLER

Date	American Bankers and Industrialists	U.S. Affiliated Firm	German Source		Intermediary for Funds/Agent
1923	Henry FORD	FORD MOTOR COMPANY			—
1931	E. R. HARRIMAN	UNION BANKING CORP	Fritz THYSSEN	250,000 RM	Bank voor Handel en Scheepvaart N.V. (Subsidiary of August Thyssen Bank)
1932-3		Flick (a director of AEG)	Friedrich FLICK	150,000 RM	Direct to NSDAP
February-March 1933		NONE	Emil KIRDORF	600,000 RM	"Nationale Treuhand" a/c at Delbrück Schickler Bank
February-March 1933	Edsel B. FORD, C.E. MITCHELL, Walter TEAGLE, Paul M. WARBURG	AMERICAN I.G.	I.G. FARBEN	400,000 RM	"Nationale Treuhand"
February-March 1933		NONE	Reichsverband der Automobilindustrie	100,000 RM	"Nationale Treuhand"
February-March 1933	Gerard SWOPE, Owen D. YOUNG, C.H. MINOR, E. Arthur BALDWIN	INTERNATIONAL GENERAL ELECTRIC 25 percent	A.E.G.	60,000 RM	"Nationale Treuhand"

Date	American Director	American Company	Percent	German Recipient	Amount	Via
February-March 1933		NONE		DEMAG	50,000 RM	
February-March 1933	Owen D. YOUNG	INTERNATIONAL GENERAL ELECTRIC	16⅔ percent	OSRAM G.m.b.H.	40,000 RM	"Nationale Treuhand"
February-March 1933	Sosthenes BEHN	I.T.T.		Telefunken	35,000 RM	"Nationale Treuhand"
February-March 1933		NONE		Karl Herrman	300,000 RM	"Nationale Treuhand"
February-March 1933		NONE		A. Steinke (Director of BYBUAG)	200,000 RM	"Nationale Treuhand"
February-March 1933		NONE		Karl Lange (Machine industry)	50,000 RM	"Nationale Treuhand"
February-March 1933		NONE		F. Springorum (Hoesch A.G.)	36,000 RM	"Nationale Treuhand"
February-March 1933	Edsel B. FORD	Ford Motor Co.		Carl BOSCH (I.G. Farben & Ford Motor A.G.)		
1932-1944	Walter TEAGLE, J.A. MOFFETT, W.S. FARISH	Standard Oil of N.J.	94 percent	Emil HELFFRICH (German-American Petroleum Co)		Heinrich Himmler S.S. via Keppler's Circle
1932-1944	Sosthenes BEHN	I.T.T.		Kurt von SCHRÖDER, Mix & Genest, Lorenz		Heinrich Himmler S.S. via Keppler's Circle

J. G. GROENINGEN	Vereinigte Stahlwerke (the steel cartel which also funded Hitler)
C. LIEVENSE	President, Union Banking Corp., New York City
E. S. JAMES	Partner Brown Brothers, later Brown Brothers, Harriman & Co.

Thyssen arranged a credit of 250,000 marks for Hitler, through this Dutch bank affiliated with the Harrimans. Thyssen's book, later repudiated, states that as much as one million marks came from Thyssen.

Thyssen's U.S. partners were, of course, prominent members of the Wall Street financial establishment. Edward Henry Harriman, the nineteenth-century railroad magnate, had two sons, W. Averell Harriman (born in 1891), and E. Roland Harriman (born in 1895). In 1917 W. Averell Harriman was a director of Guaranty Trust Company and he was involved in the Bolshevik Revolution.[16] According to his biographer, Averell started at the bottom of the career ladder as a clerk and section hand after leaving Yale in 1913, then "he moved steadily forward to positions of increasing responsibility in the fields of transportation and finance."[17] In addition to his directorship in Guaranty Trust, Harriman formed the Merchant Shipbuilding Corporation in 1917, which soon became the largest merchant fleet under American flag. This fleet was dis posed of in 1925 and Harriman entered the lucrative Russian market.[18]

In winding up these Russian deals in 1929, Averell Harriman received a windfall profit of $1 million from the usually hard-headed Soviets, who have a reputation of giving nothing away without some present or later *quid pro quo*. Concurrently with these successful moves in international finance, Averell Harriman has always been attracted by so-called "public" service. In 1913 Harriman's "public" service began with an appointment to the Palisades Park Commission. In 1933 Harriman was appointed chairman of the New York State Committee of Employment, and in 1934 became Administrative Officer of Roosevelt's NRA — the Mussolini-like brainchild of General Electric's Gerard Swope.[19] There followed a stream of "public" offices, first the Lend Lease program, then as Ambassador to the Soviet Union, later as Secretary of Commerce.

By contrast, E. Roland Harriman confined his activities to private business in international finance without venturing, as did brother Averell, into "public" service. In 1922 Roland and Averell formed W. A. Harriman & Company. Still later Roland became chairman of the board of Union Pacific Railroad and a director of *Newsweek* magazine, Mutual

Life Insurance Company of New York, a member of the board of governors of the American Red Cross, and a member of the American Museum of Natural History.

Nazi financier Hendrik Jozef Kouwenhoven, Roland Harriman's fellow-director at Union Banking Corporation in New York, was managing director of the Bank voor Handel en Scheepvaart N.V. (BHS) of Rotterdam. In 1940 the BHS held approximately $2.2 million assets in the Union Banking Corporation, which in turn did most of its business with BHS.[2] In the 1930s Kouwenhoven was also a director of the Vereinigte Stahlwerke A.G., the steel cartel founded with Wall Street funds in the mid-1920s. Like Baron Schröder, he was a prominent Hitler supporter.

Another director of the New York Union Banking Corporation was Johann Groeninger, a German subject with numerous industrial and financial affiliations involving Vereinigte Stahlwerke, the August Thyssen group, and a directorship of August Thyssen Hütte A.G.[21]

This affiliation and mutual business interest between Harriman and the Thyssen interests does not suggest that the Harrimans directly financed Hitler. On the other hand, it does show that the Harrimans were intimately connected with prominent Nazis Kouwenhoven and Groeninger and a Nazi front bank, the Bank voor Handel en Scheepvaart. There is every reason to believe that the Harrimans knew of Thyssen's support for the Nazis. In the case of the Harrimans, it is important to bear in mind their long-lasting and intimate relationship with the Soviet Union and the Harriman's position at the center of Roosevelt's New Deal and the Democratic Party. The evidence suggests that some members of the Wall Street elite are connected with, and certainly have influence with, *all* significant political groupings in the contemporary world socialist spectrum — Soviet socialism, Hitler's national socialism, and Roosevelt's New Deal socialism.

Financing Hitler in the March 1933 General Election

Putting the Georg Bell-Deterding and the Thyssen-Harriman cases to one side, we now examine the core of Hitler's backing. In May 1932 the so-called "Kaiserhof Meeting" took place between Schmitz of I.G. Farben, Max Ilgner of American I.G. Farben, Kiep of Hamburg-America Line, and Diem of the German Potash Trust. More than 500,000 marks was raised at this meeting and deposited to the credit of Rudolf Hess in the Deutsche Bank. It is noteworthy, in light of the "Warburg myth" described in Chapter Ten that Max Ilgner of the American I.G. Farben contributed 100,000 RM, or one-fifth of the total. The "Sidney Warburg" book claims Warburg involvement in the funding of Hitler, and Paul Warburg was a director of American I.G. Farben[22] while Max Warburg was a director of I.G. Farben.

There exists irrefutable documentary evidence of a further role of international bankers and industrialists in the financing of the Nazi Party and the *Volkspartie* for the March 1933 German election. A total of three million Reichmarks was subscribed by prominent firms and businessmen, suitably "washed" through an account at the Delbrück Schickler Bank, and then passed into the hands of Rudolf Hess for use by Hitler and the NSDAP. This transfer of funds was followed by the Reichstag fire, abrogation of constitutional rights, and consolidation of Nazi power. Access to the Reichstag by the arsonists was obtained through a tunnel from a house where Putzi Hanfstaengel was staying; the Reichstag fire itself was used by Hitler as a pretext to abolish constitutional rights. In brief, within a few weeks of the major funding of Hitler there was a linked sequence of major events: the financial contribution from prominent bankers and industrialists to the 1933 election, burning of the Reichstag, abrogation of constitutional rights, and subsequent seizure of power by the Nazi Party.

The fund-raising meeting was held February 20, 1933 in the home of Goering, who was then president of the Reichstag, with Hjalmar Horace Greeley Schacht acting as host. Among those present, according to I.G. Farben's von Schnitzler, were:

> *Krupp von Bohlen, who, in the beginning of 1933, was president of the Reichsverband der Deutschen Industrie Reich Association of German Industry; Dr. Albert Voegler, the leading man of the Vereinigte Stahlwerke; Von Loewenfeld; Dr. Stein, head of the Gewerkschaft Auguste-Victoria, a mine which belongs to the IG.[23]*

Hitler expounded his political views to the assembled businessmen in a lengthy two-and-one-half hour speech, using the threat of Communism and a Communist take-over to great effect:

> *It is not enough to say we do not want Communism in our economy. If we continue on our old political course, then we shall perish . . . . It is the noblest task of the leader to find ideals that are stronger than the factors that pull the people together. I*

*recognized even while in the hospital that one had to search for
new ideals conducive to reconstruction. I found them in
nationalism, in the value of personality, and in the denial of
reconciliation between nations . . . .*

*Now we stand before the last election. Regardless of the
outcome, there will be no retreat, even if the coming election
does not bring about decision, one way or another. If the election
does not decide, the decision must be brought about by other
means. I have intervened in order to give the people once more
the chance to decide their fate by themselves . . . .*

*There are only two possibilities, either to crowd back the
opponent on constitutional grounds, and for this purpose once
more this election; or a struggle will be conducted with other
weapons, which may demand greater sacrifices. I hope the
German people thus recognize the greatness of the hour.*[24]

After Hitler had spoken, Krupp von Bohlen expressed the support of
the assembled industrialists and bankers in the concrete form of a three-
million-mark political fund. It turned out to be more than enough to acquire power, because 600,000 marks remained unexpended after the election.

Hjalmar Schacht organized this historic meeting. We have previously described Schacht's links with the United States: his father was
cashier for the Berlin Branch of Equitable Assurance, and Hjalmar was
intimately involved almost on a monthly basis with Wall Street.

The largest contributor to the fund was I.G. Farben, which com-
mitted itself for 30 percent (or 500,000 marks) of the total. Director A.
Steinke, of BUBIAG (Braunkohlen-u. Brikett-Industrie A.G.), an I.G.
Farben subsidiary, personally contributed another 200,000 marks. In
brief, 45 percent of the funds for the 1933 election came from I.G. Farben.
If we look at the directors of American I.G. Farben — the U.S. subsidiary
of I.G. Farben — we get close to the roots of Wall Street involvement with
Hitler. The board of American I.G. Farben at this time contained some of
the most prestigious names among American industrialists: Edsel B. Ford
of the Ford Motor Company, C.E. Mitchell of the Federal Reserve Bank
of New York, and Walter Teagle, director of the Federal Reserve Bank of
New York, the Standard Oil Company of New Jersey, and President
Franklin D. Roosevelt's Georgia Warm Springs Foundation.

Paul M. Warburg, first director of the Federal Reserve Bank of New
York and chairman of the Bank of Manhattan, was a Farben director and

in Germany his brother Max Warburg was also a director of I.G. Farben. H. A. Metz of I.G. Farben was also a director of the Warburg's Bank of Manhattan. Finally, Carl Bosch of American I.G. Farben was also a director of Ford Motor Company A-G in Germany.

Three board members of American I.G. Farben were found guilty at the Nuremburg War Crimes Trials: Max Ilgner, F. Ter Meer, and Hermann Schmitz. As we have noted, the American board members — Edsel Ford, C. E. Mitchell, Walter Teagle, and Paul Warburg — were not placed on trial at Nuremburg, and so far as the records are concerned, it appears that they were not even questioned about their knowledge of the 1933 Hitler fund.

The 1933 Political Contributions

Who were the industrialists and bankers who placed election funds at the disposal of the Nazi Party in 1933? The list of contributors and the amount of their contribution is as follows:

FINANCIAL CONTRIBUTIONS TO HITLER: Feb. 23-Mar. 13, 1933:

(The Hjalmar Schacht account at Delbrück, Schickler Bank)

Political Contributions by Firms (with selected affiliated directors)	Amount Pledged	Percent of Firm Total
Verein fuer die Bergbaulichen Interessen (Kirdorf)	$600,000	45.8
I.G. Farbenindustrie (Edsel Ford, C.E. Mitchell, Walter Teagle, Paul Warburg)	400,000	30.5
Automobile Exhibition, Berlin (Reichsverbund der Automobilindustrie S.V.)	100,000	7.6
A.E.G., German General Electric (Gerard Swope, Owen Young, C.H. Minor, Arthur Baldwin)	60,000	4.6
Demag	50,000	3.8
Osram G.m.b.H. (Owen Young)	40,000	3.0

Telefunken Gesellschaft fuer drahtlose Telegraphie	35,000	2.7
Accumulatoren-Fabrik A.G. (Quandt of A.E.G.)	25,000	1.9
Total from industry	1,310,000	99.9

Plus Political Contributions by Individual Businessmen:

Karl Hermann	300,000
Director A. Steinke (BUBIAG- Braunkohlen—u. Brikett— Industrie A.G.)	200,000
Dir. Karl Lange (Geschaftsfuhrendes Vostandsmitglied des Vereins Deutsches Maschinenbau—Anstalten)	50,000
Dr. F. Springorum (Chairman: Eisen-und Stahlwerke Hoesch A.G.)	36,000

Source: See Appendix for translation of original document.

How can we prove that these political payments actually took place?

The payments to Hitler in this final step on the road to dictatorial Naziism were made through the private bank of Delbrück Schickler. The Delbrück Schickler Bank was a subsidiary of Metallgesellschaft A.G. ("Metall"), an industrial giant, the largest non-ferrous metal company in Germany, and the dominant influence in the world's nonferrous metal trading. The principal shareholders of "Metall" were I.G. Farben and the British Metal Corporation. We might note incidentally that the British directors on the "Metall" *Aufsichsrat* were Walter Gardner (Amalgamated Metal Corporation) and Captain Oliver Lyttelton (also on the board of Amalgamated Metal and paradoxically later in World War II to become the British Minister of Production).

There exists among the Nuremburg Trial papers the original transfer slips from the banking division of I.G. Farben and other firms listed on page 110 to the Delbrück Schickler Bank in Berlin, informing the bank of the transfer of funds from Dresdner Bank, and other banks, to their *Nationale Treuhand* (National Trusteeship) account. This account was disbursed by Rudolf Hess for Nazi Party expenses during the election. Translation of the I.G. Farben transfer slip, selected as a sample, is as follows:[25]

Translation of I.G. Farben letter of February 27, 1933, advising of transfer of 400,000 Reichsmarks to National Trusteeship account:

I.G. FARBENINDUSTRIE AKTIENGESELLSCHAFT
Bank Department

Firm: Delbrück Schickler & Co.,
BERLIN W.8
Mauerstrasse 63/65, Frankfurt (Main) 20
Our Ref: (Mention in Reply)   27 February 1933
    B./Goe.

We are informing you herewith that we have authorized the Dresdner Bank in Frankfurt/M., to pay you tomorrow forenoon: RM 400,000 which you will use in favor of the account "NATIONALE TREUHAND" (National Trusteeship).

                Respectfully,
                I.G. Farbenindustrie Aktiengesellschaft
                by Order:
                (Signed) SELCK   (Signed) BANGERT

By special delivery.[26]

At this juncture we should take note of the efforts that have been made to direct our attention away from American financiers (and German financiers connected with American-affiliated companies) who were involved with the funding of Hitler. Usually the blame for financing Hitler has been exclusively placed upon Fritz Thyssen or Emil Kirdorf. In the case of Thyssen this blame was widely circulated in a book allegedly authored by Thyssen in the middle of World War II but later repudiated by him.[27] Why Thyssen would want to admit such actions before the defeat of Naziism is unexplained.

Emil Kirdorf, who died in 1937, was always proud of his association with the rise of Naziism. The attempt to limit Hitler financing to Thyssen and Kirdorf extended into the Nuremburg trials in 1946, and was challenged only by the Soviet delegate. Even the Soviet delegate was unwilling to produce evidence of American associations; this is not surprising because the Soviet Union depends on the goodwill of these same financiers to transfer much needed advanced Western technology to the U.S.S.R.

At Nuremburg, statements were made and allowed to go unchallenged which were directly contrary to the known direct evidence presented above. For example, Buecher, Director General of German General Electric, was absolved from sympathy for Hitler:

*Thyssen has confessed his error like a man and has courage-
ously paid a heavy penalty for it. On the other side stand men
like Reusch of the Gutehoffnungshuette, Karl Bosch, the late
chairman of the I.G. Farben Aufsichtsrat, who would very likely
have come to a sad end, had he not died in time. Their feelings
were shared by the deputy chairman of the Aufsichtsrat of Kalle.
The Siemens and AEG companies which, next to I.G. Farben,
were the most powerful German concerns, and they were determined opponents of national socialism.*

*I know that this unfriendly attitude on the part of the
Siemens concern to the Nazis resulted in the firm receiving
rather rough treatment. The Director General of the AEG
(Allgemeine Elektrizitats Gesellschaft), Geheimrat Buecher,
whom I knew from my stay in the colonies, was anything but a
Nazi. I can assure General Taylor that it is certainly wrong to
assert that the leading industrialists as such favored Hitler before his seizure of power.*[28]

Yet on page 56 of this book we reproduce a document originating
with General Electric, transferring General Electric funds to the National
Trusteeship account controlled by Rudolf Hess on behalf of Hitler and
used in the 1933 elections.

Similarly, von Schnitzler, who was present at the February 1933
meeting on behalf of I.G. Farben, denied I.G. Farben's contributions to
the 1933 Nationale Treuhand:

*I never heard again of the whole matter [that of financing
Hitler], but I believe that either the buro of Goering or Schacht
or the Reichsverband der Deutschen Industrie had asked the office of Bosch or Schmitz for payment of IG's share in the elec
tion fund. As I did not take the matter up again I not even at that
time knew whether and which amount had been paid by the IG.
According to the volume of the IG, I should estimate IG's share
being something like 10 percent of the election fund, but as far
as I know there is no evidence that I.G. Farben participated in
the payments.*[29]

As we have seen, the evidence is incontrovertible regarding political
cash contributions to Hitler at the crucial point of the takeover of power in
Germany — and Hitler's earlier speech to the industrialists clearly

revealed that a coercive takeover was the premeditated intent.

We know exactly who contributed, how much, and through what channels. It is notable that the largest contributors — I.G. Farben, German General Electric (and its affiliated company Osram), and Thyssen — were affiliated with Wall Street financiers. These Wall Street financiers were at the heart of the financial elite and they were prominent in contemporary American politics. Gerard Swope of General Electric was author of Roosevelt's New Deal, Teagle was one of NRA's top administrators, Paul Warburg and his associates at American I.G. Farben were Roosevelt advisors. It is perhaps not an extraordinary coincidence that Roosevelt's New Deal — called a "fascist measure" by Herbert Hoover — should have so closely resembled Hitler's program for Germany, and that both Hitler and Roosevelt took power in the same month of the same year — March 1933.

CHAPTER EIGHT

Putzi: Friend of Hitler and Roosevelt

Ernst Sedgewick Hanfstaengl (or Hanfy or Putzi, as he was more usually called), like Hjalmar Horace Greeley Schacht, was another German-American at the core of the rise of Hitlerism. Hanfstaengl was born into a well-known New England family; he was a cousin of Civil War General John Sedgewick and a grandson of another Civil War General, William Heine. Introduced to Hitler in the early 1920s by Captain Truman-Smith, the U.S. Military Attaché in Berlin, Putzi became an ardent Hitler supporter, on occasion financed the Nazis and, according to Ambassador William Dodd, ". . . is said to have saved Hitler's life in 1923."[1]

By coincidence, S.S. leader Heinrich Himmler's father was also Putzi's form master at the Royal Bavarian Wilhelms gymnasium. Putzi's student day friends at Harvard University were "such outstanding future figures" as Walter Lippman, John Reed (who figures prominently in *Wall Street and the Bolshevik Revolution*), and Franklin D. Roosevelt. After a few years at Harvard, Putzi established the family art business in New York; it was a delightful combination of business and pleasure, for as he says, "the famous names who visited me were legion, Pierpont Morgan, Toscanini, Henry Ford, Caruso, Santos-Dumont, Charlie Chaplin, Paderewski, and a daughter of President Wilson."[2] It was also at Harvard that Putzi made friends with the future President Franklin Delano Roosevelt:

> I took most of my meals at the Harvard Club, where I made friends with the young Franklin D. Roosevelt, at that time a rising New York State Senator. Also I received several invitations to visit his distant cousin Teddy, the former President, who had retired to his estate at Sagamore Hill.[3]

From these varied friendships (or perhaps after reading this book and its predecessors, *Wall Street and FDR* and *Wall Street and the Bolshevik*

Revolution, the reader may consider Putzi's friendship to have been confined to a peculiarly elitist circle), Putzi became not only an early friend, backer and financier of Hitler, but among those early Hitler supporters he was, ". . . almost the only person who crossed the lines of his (Hitler's) groups of acquaintances."[4]

In brief, Putzi was an American citizen at the heart of th Hitler entourage from the early 1920s to the late 1930s. In 1943, after falling out of favor with the Nazis and interned by the Allies, Putzi was bailed out of the miseries of a Canadian prisoner of war camp by his friend and protector President Franklin D. Roosevelt. When FDR's actions threatened to become an internal political problem in the United States, Putzi was re-interned in England. As if it is not surprising enough to find both Heinrich Himmler and Franklin D. Roosevelt prominent in Putzi's life, we also discover that the Nazi Stormtrooper marching songs were composed by Hanfstaengl, "including the one that was played by the brownshirt columns as they marched through the Brandenburger Tor on the day Hitler took over power."[5] To top this eye-opener, Putzi averred that the genesis of the Nazi chant "Sieg Heil, Sieg Heil," used in the Nazi mass rallies, was none other than "Harvard, Harvard, Harvard, rah, rah, rah."

Putzi certainly helped finance the first Nazi daily press, the *Volkische Beobachter*. Whether he saved Hitler's life from the Communists is less verifiable, and while kept out of the actual writing process of *Mein Kampf* — much to his disgust — Putzi did have the honor to finance its publication, "and the fact that Hitler found a functioning staff when he was released from jail was entirely due to our efforts."[7]

When Hitler came to power in March 1933, simultaneously with Franklin Delano Roosevelt in Washington, a private "emissary" was sent from Roosevelt in Washington, D.C. to Hanfstaengl in Berlin, with a message to the effect that as it appeared Hitler would soon achieve power in Germany, Roosevelt hoped, in view of their long acquaintance, that Putzi would do his best to prevent any rashness and hot-headedness. "Think of your piano playing and try and use the soft pedal if things get too loud," was FDR's message. "If things start getting awkward please get in touch with our ambassador at once."[8]

Hanfstaengl kept in close touch with the American Ambassador in Berlin, William E. Dodd—apparently much to his disgust, because Putzi's recorded comments on Dodd are distinctly unflattering:

> *In many ways, he [Dodd] was an unsatisfactory represen-*
> *tative. He was a modest little Southern history professor, who*

ran his embassy on a shoestring and was probably trying to save money out of his pay. At a time when it needed a robust millionaire to compete with the flamboyance of the Nazis, he teetered around self-effacingly as if he were still on his college campus. His mind and his prejudices were small.[9]

In point of fact Ambassador Dodd pointedly tried to decline Roosevelt's Ambassadorial appointment. Dodd had no inheritance and preferred to live on his State Department pay rather than political spoils; unlike the politician Dodd was particular from whom he received money. In any event, Dodd commented equally harshly on Putzi, ". . . he gave money to Hitler in 1923, helped him write *Mein Kampf*, and was in every way familiar with Hitler's motives . . . ."

Was Hanfstaengl an agent for the Liberal Establishment in the U.S.? We can probably rule out this possibility because, according to Ladislas Farago, it was Putzi who blew the whistle on top-level British penetration of the Hitler command. Farago reports that Baron William S. de Ropp had penetrated the highest Nazi echelons in pre-World War II days and Hitler used de Ropp ". . . as his confidental consultant about British affairs."[10] De Ropp was suspected as being a double agent only by Putzi. According to Farago:

> *The only person . . . who ever suspected him of such duplicity and cautioned the Fuehrer about him was the erratic Putzi Hanfstaengl, the Harvard educated chief of Hitler's office dealing with the foreign press.*

As Farago notes, "Bill de Ropp was playing the game in both camps—a double agent at the very top."[11] Putzi was equally diligent in warning his friends, the Hermann Goerings, about potential spies in *their* camp. Witness the following extract from Putzi's memoirs, in which he points the accusing finger of espionage at the Goerings' gardener:

> *"Herman," I said one day, "I will bet any money that fellow Greinz is a police spy." "Now really, Putzi," Karin [Mrs. Herman Goering] broke in, "he's such a nice fellow and he's a wonderful gardener." "He's doing exactly what a spy ought to do," I told her, "he has made himself indispensable."*[12]

By 1941 Putzi was out of favor with Hitler and the Nazis, fled Germany, and was interned in a Canadian prisoner of war camp. With Germany and the United States now ar war Putzi re-calculated the odds and concluded, "Now I knew for certain that Germany would be defeated."[13] Putzi's release from the POW camp came with the personal intervention of old friend President Roosevelt:

> *One day a correspondent of the Hearst press named Kehoe obtained permission to visit Fort Henry. I managed to have a few words with him in a corner. "I know your boss well," I told him. "Will you do me a small service?" Fortunately he recognized my name.*
>
> *I gave him a letter, which he slipped into his pocket. It was addressed to the American Secretary of State, Cordell Hull. A few days later it was on the desk of my Harvard Club friend, Franklin Delano Roosevelt. In it I offered to act as a political and psychological warfare adviser in the war against Germany.*[14]

The response and offer to "work" for the American side was accepted. Putzi was installed in comfortable surroundings with his son, U.S. Army Sergeant Egon Hanfstaengl, also there as a personal aide. In 1944, under pressure of a Republican threat to blow the whistle on Roosevelt's favoritism for a former Nazi, Egon was shipped out to New Guinea and Putzi hustled off to England, where the British promptly interned him for the duration of the war, Roosevelt or no Roosevelt.

Putzi's Role in the Reichstag Fire

Putzi's friendships and political manipulations may or may not be of any great consequence, but his role in the Reichstag fire is significant.

The firing of the Reichstag on February 27, 1933 is one of the key events of modern times. The fire was used by Adolf Hitler to claim imminent Communist revolution, suspend constitutional rights, and seize totalitarian power. From that point on there was no turning back for Germany; the world was set upon the course to World War II.

At the time the firing of the Reichstag was blamed on the Communists, but there is little question in historical perspective that the fire was deliberately set by the Nazis to provide an excuse to seize political power. Fritz Thyssen commented in the post-war Dustbin interrogations:

> *When the Reichstag was burned, everyone was sure it had been done by the communists. I later learned in Switzerland that it was all a lie.*[15]

*Schacht states quite emphatically:

> *Nowadays it would be quite clear that this action could not be fastened on the Communist Party. To what extent individual National Socialists co-operated in the planning and execution of the deed will be difficult to establish, but in view of all that has been revealed in the meantime, the fact must be accepted that Goebbels and Goering each played a leading part, the one in planning, the other in carrying out the plan.*[16]

The Reichstag fire was deliberately set, probably utilizing a flammable liquid, by a group of experts. This is where Putzi Hanfstaengl comes into the picture. The key question is how did this group, bent on arson, gain access to the Reichstag to do the job? After 8 p.m. only one door in the main building was unlocked and this door was guarded. Just before 9 p.m. a tour of the building by watchmen indicated all was well; no flammable liquids were noticed and nothing was out of the ordinary in the Sessions Chamber where the fire started. Apparently no one could have gained access to the Reichstag building after 9 p.m., and no one was seen to enter or leave between 9 p.m. and the start of the fire.

There was only one way a group with flammable materials could have entered the Reichstag — through a tunnel that ran between the Reichstag and the Palace of the Reichstag President. Hermann Goering was president of the Reichstag and lived in the Palace, and numerous S.A. and S.S. men were known to be in the Palace. In the words of one author:

> *The use of the underground passage, with all its complications, was possible only to National-Socialists, the advance and escape of the incendiary gang was feasible only with the connivance of highly-placed employees of the Reichstag. Every clue, every probability points damningly in one direction, to the conclusion that the burning of the Reichstag was the work of National-Socialists.*[17]

How does Putzi Hanfstaengl fit into this picture of arson and political intrigue?

Putzi — by his own admission — was in the Palace room at the other end of the tunnel leading to the Reichstag. And according to *The Reichstag Fire Trial*, Putzi Hanfstaengl was actually in the Palace itself during the fire:

> *Hanfstaengl directed operations within the Palace, the*

propaganda apparatus stood ready, and the leaders of the Storm Troopers were in their places. With the official bulletins planned in advance, the orders of arrest prepared, Karwahne, Frey and Kroyer waiting patiently in their cafe, the preparations were complete, the scheme almost perfect.[18]

Dimitrov also asserts that:

The National-Socialist leaders, Hitler, Goering and Goebbels, together with the high National-Socialist officials, Daluege, Hanfstaengl and Albrecht, happened to be present in Berlin on the day of the fire, despite that the election campaign was at its highest pitch throughout Germany, six days before the poll. Goering and Goebbels, under oath, furnished contradictory explanations for their "fortuitous" presence in Berlin with Hitler on that day. The National-Socialist Hanfstaengl, as Goering's "guest," was present in the Palace of the Reichstag President, immediately adjacent to the Reichstag, at the time when the fire broke out, although his "host" was not there at that time.[19]

According to Nazi Kurt Ludecke, there once existed a document signed by S.A. Leader Karl Ernst — who supposedly set the fire and was later murdered by fellow Nazis — which implicated Goering, Goebbels, and Hanfstaengl in the conspiracy.

Roosevelt's New Deal and Hitler's New Order

Hjalmar Schacht challenged his post-war Nuremburg interrogators with the observation that Hitler's New Order program was the same as Roosevelt's New Deal program in the United States. The interrogators understandably snorted and rejected the observation. However, a little research suggests that not only are the two programs quite similar in content, but that Germans had no trouble in observing the similarities. There is in the Roosevelt Library a small book presented to FDR by Dr. Helmut Magers in December 1933.[20] On the flyleaf of this presentation copy is written the inscription,

To the President of the United States, Franklin D. Roosevelt, in profound admiration of his conception of a new economic order and with devotion for his personality. The author, Baden, Germany, November 9, 1933.

FDR's reply to this admiration for his new economic order was as follows:[21]

> *(Washington) December 19, 1933*
>
> *My dear Dr. Magers: I want to send you my thanks for the copy of your little book about me and the "New Deal." Though, as you know, I went to school in Germany and could speak German with considerable fluency at one time, I am reading your book not only with great interest but because it will help my German.*
>
> *Very sincerely yours,*

The New Deal or the "new economic order" was not a creature of classical liberalism. It was a creature of corporate socialism. Big business as reflected in Wall Street strived for a state order in which they could control industry and eliminate competition, and this was the heart of FDR's New Deal. General Electric, for example, is prominent in both Nazi Germany and the New Deal. German General Electric was a prominent financier of Hitler and the Nazi Party, and A.E.G. also financed Hitler both directly and indirectly through Osram. International General Electric in New York was a major participant in the ownership and direction of both A.E.G. and Osram. Gerard Swope, Owen Young, and A. Baldwin of General Electric in the United States were directors of A.E.G. However, the story does not stop at General Electric and financing of Hitler in 1933.

In a previous book, *Wall Street and the Bolshevik Revolution*, the author identified the role of General Electric in the Bolshevik Revolution and the geographic location of American participants as at 120 Broadway, New York City; the executive offices of General Electric were also at 120 Broadway. When Franklin Delano Roosevelt was working in Wall Street, his address was also 120 Broadway. In fact, Georgia Warm Springs Foundation, the FDR Foundation, was located at 120 Broadway. The prominent financial backer of an early Roosevelt Wall Street venture from 120 Broadway was Gerard Swope of General Electric. And it was "Swope's Plan" that became Roosevelt's New Deal — the fascist plan that Herbert Hoover was unwilling to foist on the United States. In brief, both Hitler's New Order and Roosevelt's New Deal were backed by the same industrialists and in content were quite similar — *i.e.*, they were both plans for a corporate state.

There were then both corporate and individual bridges between FDR's America and Hitler's Germany. The first bridge was the American

I.G. Farben, American affiliate of I.G. Farben, the largest German corporation. On the board of American I.G. sat Paul Warburg, of the Bank of Manhattan and the Federal Reserve Bank of New York. The second bridge was between International General Electric, a wholly owned subsidiary of General Electric Company and its partly owned affiliate in Germany, A.E.G. Gerard Swope, who formulated FDR's New Deal, was chairman of I.G.E. and on the board of A.E.G. The third "bridge" was between Standard Oil of New Jersey and Vacuum Oil and its wholly owned German subsidiary, Deutsche-Amerikanische Gesellschaft. The chairman of Standard Oil of New Jersey was Walter Teagle, of the Federal Reserve Bank of New York. He was a trustee of Franklin Delano Roosevelt's Georgia Warm Springs Foundation and appointed by FDR to a key administrative post in the National Recovery Administration.

These corporations were deeply involved in both the promotion of Roosevelt's New Deal and the construction of the military power of Nazi Germany. Putzi Hanfstaengl's role in the early days, up to the mid-1930s anyway, was an informal link between the Nazi elite and the White House. After the mid-1930s, when the world was set on the course for war, Putzi's importance declined — while American Big Business continued to be represented through such intermediaries as Baron Kurt von Schröder attorney Westrick, and membership in Himmler's Circle of Friends.

CHAPTER NINE

Wall Street and the Nazi Inner Circle

During the entire period of our business contacts we had no inkling of Farben's conniving part in Hitler's brutal policies. We offer any help we can give to see that complete truth is brought to light and that rigid justice is done. (F.W. Abrams, Chairman of the Board, Standard Oil of New Jersey, 1946.)

Adolf Hitler, Hermann Goering, Josef Goebbels, and Heinrich Himmler, the inner group of Naziism, were at the same time heads of minor fiefdoms within the Nazi State. Power groups or political cliques were centered around these Nazi leaders, more importantly after the late 1930s around Adolf Hitler and Heinrich Himmler, Reich-Leader of the S.S. (the dreaded *Schutzstaffel*). The most important of these Nazi inner circles was created by order of the Fuehrer; it was known first as the Keppler Circle and later as Himmler's Circle of Friends.

The Keppler Circle originated as a group of German businessmen supporting Hitler's rise to power before and during 1933. In the mid-1930s the Keppler Circle came under the influence and protection of S.S. chief Himmler and the organizational control of Cologne banker and prominent Nazi businessman Kurt von Schröder. Schröder, it will be recalled, was head of the J.H. Stein Bank in Germany and affiliated with the J. Henry Schroder Banking Corporation of New York. It is within this innermost of the inner circles, the very core of Naziism, that we find Wall Street, including Standard Oil of New Jersey and I.T.T., represented from 1933 to as late as 1944.

Wilhelm Keppler, founder of the original Circle of Friends, typifies the well-known phenomenon of a politicized businessman — *i.e.*, a businessman who cultivates the political arena rather than the impartial market place for his profits. Such businessmen have been interested in promoting socialist causes, because a planned socialist society provides a most lucrative opportunity for contracts through political influence.

Scenting such profitable opportunities, Keppler joined the national socialists and was close to Hitler before 1933. The Circle of Friends grew out of a meeting between Adolf Hitler and Wilhelm Keppler in December 1931. During the course of their conversation — this was several years before Hitler became dictator — the future Fuehrer expressed a wish to have reliable German businessmen available for economic advice when the Nazis took power. "Try to get a few economic leaders — they need not be Party members — who will be at our disposal when we come into power."[1] This Keppler undertook to do.

In March 1933 Keppler was elected to the Reichstag and became Hitler's financial expert. This lasted only briefly. Keppler was replaced by the infinitely more capable Hjalmar Schacht, and sent to Austria where in 1938 he became Reichs Commissioner, but still able to use his position to acquire considerable power in the Nazi State. Within a few years he captured a string of lucrative directorships in German firms, including chairman of the board of two I.G. Farben subsidiaries: Braunkohle-Benzin A.G. and Kontinental Oil A.G. Braunkohle-Benzin was the German exploiter of the Standard Oil of New Jersey technology for production of gasoline from coal. (See Chapter Four.)

In brief, Keppler was the chairman of the very firm that utilized American technology for the indispensible synthetic gasoline which enabled the Wehrmacht to go to war in 1939. This is significant because, when linked with other evidence presented in this chapter, it suggests that the profits and control of these fundamentally important technologies for German military ends were retained by a small group of international firms and businessmen operating across national borders.

Keppler's nephew, Fritz Kranefuss, under his uncle's protection, also gained prominence both as Adjutant to S.S. Chief Heinrich Himmler and as a businessman and political operator. It was Kranefuss' link with Himmler which led to the Keppler circle gradually drawing away from Hitler in the 1930s to come within Himmler's orbit, where in exchange for annual donations to Himmler's pet S.S. projects Circle members received political favors and not inconsiderable protection from the S.S.

Baron Kurt von Schröder was, as we have noted, the I.T.T. representative in Nazi Germany and an early member of the Keppler Circle. The original Keppler Circle consisted of:

THE ORIGINAL (PRE-1932) MEMBERS OF THE KEPPLER CIRCLE

Circle Member	Main Associations
Wilhelm KEPPLER	Chairman of I.G. Farben subsidiary Braunkohle-Benzin A.G. (exploited Standard Oil of N.J. oil from coal technology)
Fritz KRANEFUSS	Keppler's nephew and Adjutant to Heinrich Himmler. On Vorstand of BRABAG.
Kurt von SCHRÖDER	On board of all International Telephone & Telegraph subsidiaries in Germany.
Karl Vincenz KROGMANN	Lord Mayor of Hamburg
August ROSTERG	General Director of WINTERSHALL
Emil MEYER	On the board of I.T.T. subsidiaries and German General Electric.
Otto STEINBRINCK	Vice president of VEREINIGTE STAHLWERKE (steel cartel founded with Wall Street loans in 1926)
Hjalmar SCHACHT	President of the REICHSBANK
Emil HELFFRICH	Board chairman of GERMAN-AMERICAN PETROLEUM CO. (94-percent owned by Standard Oil of New Jersey) (See above under Wilhelm Keppler)
Friedrich REINHARDT	Board chairman COMMERZBANK
Ewald HECKER	Board chairman of ILSEDER HUTTE
Graf von BISMARCK	Government president of STETTIN

The S.S. Circle of Friends

This original Circle of Friends met with Hitler in May 1932 and heard a statement of Nazi objectives. Heinrich Himmler then became a frequent participant in the meetings, and through Himmler, various S.S. officers as well as other businessmen joined the group. This expanded group in time became Himmler's Circle of Friends, with Himmler acting as protector and expeditor for its members.

Consequently, banking and industrial interests — including American interests — were heavily represented in the inner circle of Naziism, and their pre-1933 financial contributions to Hitlerism which we have earlier enumerated were amply repaid. Of the "Big Five" German banks, the Dresdner Bank had the closest connections with the Nazi Party: at least a dozen members of Dresdner Bank's board of directors had high Nazi rank and no fewer than seven Dresdner Bank directors were among Keppler's expanded Circle of Friends, which never exceeded 40.

When we examine the names comprising both the original pre-1933 Keppler Circle and the post-1933 expanded Keppler and Himmler's Circle, we find the Wall Street multi-nationals heavily represented — more so than any other institutional group. Let us take each Wall Street multinational or its German associate in turn — those identified in Chapter Seven as linked to financing Hitler — and examine their links to Keppler and Heinrich Himmler.

I.G. Farben and the Keppler Circle

I.G. Farben was heavily represented within the Keppler Circle: no fewer than eight out of the peak circle membership of 40 were directors of I.G. Farben or a Farben subsidiary. These eight members included the previously described Wilhelm Keppler and his nephew Kranefuss, in addition to Baron Kurt von Schröder. The Farben presence was emphasized by member Hermann Schmitz, chairman of I.G. Farben and a director of Vereinigte Stahlwerke, both cartels built and consolidated by the Wall Street loans of the 1920s. A U.S. Congressional report described Hermann Schmitz as follows:

> *Hermann Schmitz, one of the most important persons in Germany, has achieved outstanding success simultaneously in the three separate fields, industry, finance, and government, and has served with zeal and devotion every government in power. He symbolizes the German citizen who out of the devastation of the First World War made possible the Second.*
>
> *Ironically, his may be said to be the greater guilt in that in 1919 he was a member of the Reich's peace delegation, and in the 1930's was in a position to teach the Nazis much that they had to know concerning economic penetration, cartel uses, synthetic materials for war.*[2]

Another Keppler Circle member on the I.G. Farben board was Friedrich Flick, creator of the steel cartel Vereinigte Stahlwerke and a director of Allianz Versicherungs A.G. and German General Electric (A.E.G.).

Heinrich Schmidt, a director of Dresdner Bank and chairman of the board of I.G. Farben subsidiary Braunkohle-Benzin A.G., was in the circle; so was Karl Rasche, another director of the Dresdner Bank and a director of Metallgesellschaft (parent of the Delbrück Schickler Bank) and Accumulatoren-Fabriken A.G. Heinrich Buetefisch was also a director of I.G. Farben and a member of the Keppler Circle. In brief, the I.G. Farben contribution to Rudolf Hess' Nationale Treuhand — the political slush fund — was confirmed after the 1933 takeover by heavy representation in the Nazi inner circle.

How many of these Keppler Circle members in the I.G. Farben complex were affiliated with Wall Street?

MEMBERS OF THE ORIGINAL KEPPLER CIRCLE ASSOCIATED WITH U.S. MULTI-NATIONALS

Member of Keppler Circle	I.G. Farben	I.T.T.	Standard Oil of New Jersey	General Electric
Wilhelm KEPPLER	Chairman of Farben subsidiary BRABAG		—	
Fritz KRANEFUSS	On Aufsichrat of BRABAG		—	
Emil Heinrich MEYER		On board of all I.T.T. German subsidiaries: Standard/Mix & Genest/Lorenz	—	Board of A.E.G.
Emil HELFFRICH			Chairman of DAPAG (94-percent owned by Standard of New Jersey)	
Friedrich FLICK	I.G. Farben			Board of A.E.G.
Kurt von SCHRÖDER		On board of all I.T.T. subsidiaries in Germany	—	

Similarly, we can identify other Wall Street institutions represented in the early Keppler's Circle of Friends, confirming their monetary contributions to the National Trusteeship Fund operated by Rudolf Hess on behalf of Adolf Hitler. These representatives were Emil Heinrich Meyer and banker Kurt von Schröder on the boards of all the I.T.T. subsidiaries in Germany, and Emil Helffrich, the board chairman of DAPAG, 94-percent owned by Standard Oil of New Jersey.

Wall Street in the S.S. Circle

Major U.S. multi-nationals were also very well represented in the later Heinrich Himmler Circle and made cash contributions to the S.S. (the Sonder Konto S) up to 1944 — while World War II was in progress.

Almost a quarter of the 1944 Sonder Konto S contributions came from subsidiaries of International Telephone and Telegraph, represented by Kurt von Schröder. The 1943 payments from I.T.T. subsidiaries to the Special Account were as follows:

Mix & Genest A.G.	5,000 RM
C. Lorenz AG	20,000 RM
Felten & Guilleaume	25,000 RM
Kurt von Schröder	16,000 RM

And the 1944 payments were:

Mix & Genest A.G.	5,000 RM
C. Lorenz AG	20,000 RM
Felten & Guilleaume	20,000 RM
Kurt von Schröder	16,000 RM

Sosthenes Behn of International Telephone and Telegraph transferred wartime control of Mix & Genest, C. Lorenz, and the other Standard Telephone interests in Germany to Kurt von Schröder — who was a founding member of the Keppler Circle and organizer and treasurer of Himmler's Circle of Friends. Emil H. Meyer, S.S. Untersturmfuehrer, member of the Vorstand of the Dresdner Bank, A.E.G., and a director of all the I.T.T. subsidiaries in Germany, was also a member of the Himmler Circle of Friends — giving I.T.T. two powerful representatives at the heart of the S.S.

A letter to fellow member Emil Meyer from Baron von Schröder dated February 25, 1936 describes the purposes and requirements of the Himmler Circle and the long-standing nature of the Special Account 'S' with funds at Schröder's own bank — the J.H. Stein Bank of Cologne:

Berlin, 25 February 1936
(Illegible handwriting)

To Prof. Dr. Emil H. Meyer
S.S. (Untersturmfuchrer) (second lieutenant) Member of the Managing
Board (Vorstand) of the Dresdner Bank
Berlin W. 56,
Behrenstr. 38

Personal!

To the Circle of Friends of the Reich Leader SS

At the end of the 2 day's inspection tour of Munich to which the Reich Leader SS had invited us last January, the Circle of Friends agreed to put — each one according to his means — at the Reich Leader's disposal into "Special Account S" (SonderKonto S), to be established at the banking firm J.H. Stein in Cologne, funds which are to be used for certain tasks outside of the budget. This should enable the Reich Leader to rely on all his friends. In Munich it was decided that the undersigned would make themselves available for setting up and handling this account. In the meantime the account was set up and we want every participant to know that in case he wants to make contributions to the Reich Leader for the aforementioned tasks — either on behalf of his firm or the Circle of Friends — payments may be made to the banking firm J.H. Stein, Cologne (Clearing Account of the Reich Bank, Postal Checking Acount No. 1392) to the Special Account S.

Heil Hitler!

(Signed) Kurt Baron von Schröder
(Signed) Steinbrinck[3]

This letter also explains why U.S. Army Colonel Bogdan, formerly of the Schroder Banking Corporation in New York, was anxious to divert the attention of post-war U.S. Army investigators away from the J. H. Stein Bank in Cologne to the "bigger banks" of Nazi Germany. It was the Stein Bank that held the secrets of the associations of American subsidiaries with Nazi authorities while World War II was in progress. The New York financial interests could not know the precise nature of these transactions (and particularly the nature of any records that may have been kept by their German associates), but they knew that *some* record could well exist of their war-time dealings — enough to embarrass them with the American public. It was this possibility that Colonel Bogdan tried unsuccessfully to head off.

German General Electric profited greatly from its association with Himmler and other leading Nazis. Several members of the Schröder clique were directors of A.E.G., the most prominent being Robert Pferdmenges, who was not only a member of the Keppler or Himmler Circles but was a partner in the aryanized banking house Pferdmenges & Company, the successor to the former Jewish banking house Sal Oppenheim of Cologne. Waldemar von Oppenheim achieved the dubious distinction (for a German Jew) of "honorary Aryan" and was able to continue his old established banking house under Hitler in partnership with Pferdmenges.

MEMBERS OF THE HIMMLER CIRCLE OF FRIENDS WHO WERE ALSO DIRECTORS OF AMERICAN-AFFILIATED FIRMS:

	I.G. Farben	I.T.T.	A.E.G.	Standard Oil of New Jersey
KRANEFUSS, Fritz	x			
KEPPLER, Wilhelm	x			
SCHRÖDER, Kurt Von	x	x		
BUETEFISCH, Heinrich	x			
RASCHE, Dr. Karl	x			
FLICK, Friedrich	x		x	
LINDEMANN, Karl				x
SCHMIDT, Heinrich	x			
ROEHNERT, Kellmuth			x	
SCHMIDT, Kurt			x	
MEYER, Dr. Emil		x		
SCHMITZ, Hermann	x			

Pferdmenges was also a director of A.E.G. and used his Nazi influence to good advantage.[4]

Two other directors of German General Electric were members of Himmler's Circle of Friends and made 1943 and 1944 monetary contributions to the Sonder Konto S. These were:

Friedrich Flick	100,000 RM
Otto Steinbrinck (a Flick associate)	100,000 RM

Kurt Schmitt was chairman of the board of directors of A.E.G. and a member of the Himmler Circle of Friends, but Schmitt's name is not recorded in the list of payments for 1943 or 1944.

Chart 9-1: Wall Street Representation in the Keppler and Himmler Circles, 1933 and 1944.

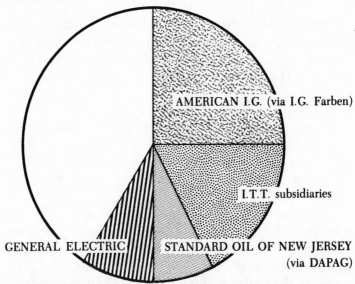

AMERICAN I.G. (via I.G. Farben)

I.T.T. subsidiaries

GENERAL ELECTRIC

STANDARD OIL OF NEW JERSEY (via DAPAG)

WALL STREET REPRESENTATION IN KEPPLER'S CIRCLE OF FRIENDS
(based on Keppler's statement of membership in 1933)

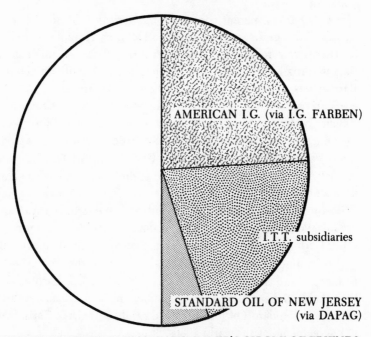

AMERICAN I.G. (via I.G. FARBEN)

I.T.T. subsidiaries

STANDARD OIL OF NEW JERSEY (via DAPAG)

WALL STREET REPRESENTATION IN HIMMLER'S CIRCLE OF FRIENDS
1944 (based on 1944 contributions to the Himmler Fund)

Standard Oil of New Jersey also made a significant contribution to Himmler's Special Account through its wholly owned (94 percent) German subsidiary, Deutsche-Amerikanische Gesellschaft (DAG). In 1943 and 1944 DAG contributed as follows:

Staatsrat Helfferich of Deutsch- Amerikanische Petroleum A.G.	10,000 RM
Staatsrat Lindemann of Deutsch- Amerikanische Petroleum A.G.	10,000 RM
and personally	4,000 RM

It is important to note that Staatsrat Lindemann contributed 4,000 RM *personally*, thus making a clear distinction between the corporate contribution of 10,000 RM from Standard Oil of New Jersey's wholly owned subsidiary and the personal contribution from director Lindemann. In the case of Staatsrat Helffrich, the only contribution was the Standard Oil contribution of 10,000 RM; there is no recorded personal donation.

I.G. Farben, parent company of American I.G. (see Chapter Two), was another significant contributor to Heinrich Himmler's Sonder Konto S. There were four I.G. Farben directors within the inner circle: Karl Rasche, Fritz Kranefuss, Heinrich Schmidt, and Heinrich Buetefisch. Karl Rasche was a member of the management committee of the Dresdner Bank and a specialist in international law and banking. Under Hitler Karl Rasche became a prominent director of many German corporations, including Accumulatoren-Fabrik A.G. in Berlin, which financed Hitler; the Metallgesellschaft; and Felten & Guilleame, an I.T.T. company. Fritz Kranefuss was a member of the board of directors of Dresdner Bank and a director of several corporations besides I.G. Farben. Kranefuss, nephew of Wilhelm Keppler, was a lawyer and prominent in many Nazi public organizations. Heinrich Schmidt, a director of I.G. Farben and several other German companies, was also a director of the Dresdner Bank.

It is important to note that all three of the above — Rasche, Kranefuss, and Schmidt — were directors of an I.G. Farben subsidiary, Braunkohle-Benzin A.G. — the manufacturer of German synthetic gasoline using Standard Oil technology, a result of the I.G. Farben-Standard Oil agreements of the early 1930s.

In brief, the Wall Street financial elite was well represented in both the early Keppler Circle and the later Himmler Circle.[5]

CHAPTER TEN

The Myth of "Sidney Warburg"

A vital question, only partly resolved, is the extent to which Hitler's accession to power in 1933 was aided *directly* by Wall Street financiers. We have shown with original documentary evidence that there was *indirect* American participation and support through German affiliated firms, and (as for example in the case of I.T.T.) there was a knowledgeable and deliberate effort to benefit from the support of the Nazi regime. Was this indirect financing extended to direct financing?

After Hitler gained power, U.S. firms and individuals worked on behalf of Naziism and certainly profited from the Nazi state. We know from the diaries of William Dodd, the American Ambassador to Germany, that in 1933 a stream of Wall Street bankers and industrialists filed through the U.S. Embassy in Berlin, expressing their admiration for Adolf Hitler — and anxious to find ways to do business with the new totalitarian regime. For example, on September 1, 1933 Dodd recorded that Henry Mann of the National City Bank and Winthrop W. Aldrich of the Chase Bank both met with Hitler and "these bankers feel they can work with him."[1] Ivy Lee, the Rockefeller public relations agent, according to Dodd "showed himself at once a capitalist and an advocate of Fascism."[2]

So at least we can identify a sympathetic response to the new Nazi dictatorship, reminiscent of the manner in which Wall Street international bankers greeted the new Russia of Lenin and Trotsky in 1917.

Who Was "Sidney Warburg"?

The question posed in this chapter is the accusation that some Wall Street financiers (the Rockefellers and Warburgs specifically have been accused) directly planned and financed Hitler's takeover in 1933, and that they did this from Wall Street. On this question the so-called myth of "Sidney Warburg" is relevant. Prominent Nazi Franz von Papen has stated in his *Memoirs*:[3]

*. . . the most documented account of the National Socialists'
sudden acquisition of funds was contained in a book published in
Holland in 1933, by the old established Amsterdam publishing
house of Van Holkema & Warendorf, called* De Geldbronnen
van Het Nationaal-Socialisme (Drie Gesprekken Met Hitler)
under the name "Sidney Warburg."

A book with this title in Dutch by "Sidney Warburg" was indeed
published in 1933, but remained on the book stalls in Holland only for a
matter of days. The book was purged.⁴ One of three surviving original copies was translated into English. The translation was at one time
deposited in the British Museum, but is now withdrawn from public circulation and is unavailable for research. Nothing is now known of the original Dutch copy upon which this English translation was based.

The second Dutch copy was owned by Chancellor Schussnigg in
Austria, and nothing is known of its present whereabouts. The third Dutch
copy found its way to Switzerland and was translated into German. The
German translation has survived down to the present day in the
Schweizerischen Sozialarchiv in Zurich, Switzerland. A certified copy of
the authenticated German translation of this Swiss survivor was purchased by the author in 1971 and translated into English. It is upon this
English translation of the German translation that the text in this chapter
is based.

Publication of the "Sidney Warburg" book was duly reported in the
New York Times (November 24, 1933) under the title "Hoax on Nazis
Feared." A brief article noted that a "Sidney Warburg" pamphlet has
appeared in Holland, and the author is not the son of Felix Warburg. The
translator is J. G. Shoup, a Belgian newspaperman living in Holland. The
publishers and Shoup "are wondering if they have not been the victims of
a hoax." The *Times* account adds:

> *The pamphlet repeats an old story to the effect that leading
> Americans, including John D. Rockefeller, financed Hitler from
> 1929 to 1932 to the extent of $32,000,000, their motive being "to
> liberate Germany from the financial grip of France by bringing
> about a revolution." Many readers of the pamphlet have pointed
> out that it contains many inaccuracies.*

Why was the Dutch original withdrawn from circulation in 1933? Because "Sidney Warburg" did not exist and a "Sidney Warburg" was
claimed as the author. Since 1933 the "Sidney Warburg" book has been

promoted by various parties both as a forgery and as a genuine document. The Warburg family itself has gone to some pains to substantiate its falsity.

What does the book report? What does the book claim happened in Germany in the early 1930s? And do these events have any resemblance to facts we know to be true from other evidence?

From the viewpoint of research methodology it is much more preferable to assume that the "Sidney Warburg" book *is* a forgery, unless we can prove the contrary. This is the procedure we shall adopt. The reader may well ask — then why bother to look closely at a possible forgery? There are at least two good reasons, apart from academic curiosity.

First, the Warburg claim that the book is a forgery has a curious and vital flaw. The Warburgs deny as false a book they admit not to have read — nor even seen. The Warburg denial is limited specifically to non-authorship by a Warburg. This denial is acceptable; but it does not deny or reject the validity of the *contents*. The denial merely repudiates authorship.

Second, we have already identified I.G. Farben as a key financier and backer of Hitler. We have provided photographic evidence (page 64) of the bank transfer slip for 400,000 marks from I.G. Farben to Hitler's "Nationale Treuhand" political slush fund account administered by Rudolf Hess. Now it is probable, almost certain, that "Sidney Warburg" did not exist. On the other hand, it *is* a matter of public record that the Warburgs were closely connected with I.G. Farben in Germany and the United States. In Germany Max Warburg was a director of I.G. Farben and in the United States brother Paul Warburg (father of James Paul Warburg) was a director of American I.G. Farben. In brief, we have incontrovertible evidence that *some* Warburgs, including the father of James Paul, the denouncer of the "Sidney Warburg" book, *were* directors of I.G. Farben. And I.G. Farben is known to have financed Hitler. "Sidney Warburg" was a myth, but I.G. Farben directors Max Warburg and Paul Warburg were not myths. This is reason enough to push further.

Let us first summarize the book which James Paul Warburg claims is a forgery.

A Synopsis of the Suppressed "Sidney Warburg" Book

The Financial Sources of National Socialism opens with an alleged conversation between "Sidney Warburg" and joint author/translator I. G.

Shoup. "Warburg" relates why he was handing Shoup an English lan
guage manuscript for translation into Dutch and publication in Holland
In the words of the mythical "Sidney Warburg":

> There are moments when I want to turn away from a world
> of such intrigue, trickery, swindling and tampering with the
> stock exchange . . . . Do you know what I can never under
> stand? How it is possible that people of good and honest
> character — for which I have ample proof — participate in
> swindling and fraud, knowing full well that it will affect
> thousands.

Shoup then describes "Sidney Warburg" as "son of one of the largest
bankers in the United States, member of the banking firm Kuhn, Loeb &
Co., New York." "Sidney Warburg" then tells Shoup that he ("Warburg") wants to record for history how national socialism was financed by
New York financiers.

The first section of the book is entitled simply "1929." It relates that
in 1929 Wall Street had enormous credits outstanding in Germany and
Austria, and that these claims had, for the most part, been frozen. While
France was economically weak and feared Germany, France was also
getting the "lion's share" of reparations funds which were actually financed from the United States. In June 1929, a meeting took place
between the members of the Federal Reserve Bank and leading American
bankers to decide what to do about France, and particularly to check her
call on German reparations. This meeting was attended (according to the
"Warburg" book) by the directors of Guaranty Trust Company, the
"Presidents" of the Federal Reserve Banks, in addition to five independent bankers, "young Rockefeller," and Glean from Royal Dutch
Shell. Carter and Rockefeller according to the text "dominated the
proceedings. The others listened and nodded their heads."

The general concensus at the bankers' meeting was that the only way
to free Germany from French financial clutches was by revolution, either
Communist or German Nationalist. At an earlier meeting it had previously
been agreed to contact Hitler to "try to find out if he were amenable to
American financial support." Now Rockefeller reportedly had more
recently seen a German-American leaflet about the Hitler national
socialist movement and the purpose of this second meeting was to determine if "Sidney Warburg" was prepared to go to Germany as a courier to
make personal contact with Hitler.

In return for proferred financial support, Hitler would be expected to conduct an "aggressive foreign policy and stir up the idea of revenge against France." This policy, it was anticipated, would result in a French appeal to the United States and England for assistance in "international questions involving the eventual German aggression." Hitler was not to know about the purpose of Wall Street's assistance. It would be left "to his reason and resourcefulness to discover the motives behind the proposal." "Warburg" accepted the proposed mission and left New York for Cherbourg on the *Ile de France*, "with a diplomatic passport and letters of recommendation from Carter, Tommy Walker, Rockefeller, Glean and Herbert Hoover."

Apparently, "Sidney Warburg" had some difficulty in meeting Hitler. The American Consul in Munich did not succeed in making contact with the Nazis, and finally Warburg went directly to Mayor Deutzberg of Munich, "with a recommendation from the American Consul," and a plea to guide Warburg to Hitler. Shoup then presents extracts from Hitler's statements at this initial meeting. These extracts include the usual Hitlerian anti-Semitic rantings, and it should be noted that all the anti-Semitic parts in the "Sidney Warburg" book are spoken by Hitler. (This is important because James Paul Warburg claims the Shoup book is totally anti-Semitic.) Funding of the Nazis was discussed at this meeting and Hitler is reported to insist that funds could not be deposited in a German bank but only in a foreign bank at his disposal. Hitler asked for 100 million marks and suggested that "Sidney Warburg" report on the Wall Street reaction through von Heydt at Lutzow-ufer, 18 Berlin.[5]

After reporting back to Wall Street, Warburg learned that $24 million was too much for the American bankers; they offered $10 million. Warburg contacted von Heydt and a further meeting was arranged, this time with an "undistinguished looking man, introduced to me under the name Frey." Instructions were given to make $10 million available at the Mendelsohn & Co. Bank in Amsterdam, Holland. Warburg was to ask the Mendelsohn Bank to make out checks in marks payable to named Nazis in ten German cities. Subsequently, Warburg travelled to Amsterdam, completed his mission with Mendelsohn & Co., then went to Southampton, England and took the *Olympia* back to New York where he reported to Carter at Guaranty Trust Company. Two days later Warburg gave his report to the entire Wall Street group, but "this time an English representative was there sitting next to Glean from Royal Dutch, a man named Angell, one of the heads of the Asiatic Petroleum Co." Warburg was questioned about Hitler, and "Rockefeller showed unusual interest in Hitler's statements about the Communists."

A few weeks after Warburg's return from Europe the Hearst newspapers showed "unusual interest" in the new German Nazi Party and even the *New York Times* carried regular short reports of Hitler's speeches. Previously these newspapers had not shown too much interest, but that now changed.[6] Also, in December 1929 a long study of the German National Socialist movement appeared "in a monthly publication at Harvard University."

Part II of the suppressed "Financial Sources of National Socialism" is entitled "1931" and opens with a discussion of French influence on international politics. It avers that Herbert Hoover promised Pierre Laval of France not to resolve the debt question without first consulting the French government and [writes Shoup]:

> *When Wall Street found out about this Hoover lost the respect of this circle at one blow. Even the subsequent elections were affected — many believed that Hoover's failure to get reelected can be traced back to the issue.*[7]

In October 1931, Warburg received a letter from Hitler which he passed on to Carter at Guaranty Trust Company, and subsequently another bankers' meeting was called at the Guaranty Trust Company offices. Opinions at this meeting were divided. "Sidney Warburg" reported that Rockefeller, Carter, and McBean were for Hitler, while the other financiers were uncertain. Montague Norman of the Bank of England and Glean of Royal Dutch Shell argued that the $10 million already spent on Hitler was too much, that Hitler would never act. The meeting finally agreed in principle to assist Hitler further, and Warburg again undertook a courier assignment and went back to Germany.

On this trip Warburg reportedly discussed German affairs with "a Jewish banker" in Hamburg, with an industrial magnate, and other Hitler supporters. One meeting was with banker von Heydt and a "Luetgebrunn." The latter stated that the Nazi storm troopers were incompletely equipped and the S.S. badly needed machine guns, revolvers, and carbines.

In the next Warburg-Hitler meeting, Hitler argued that "the Soviets cannot miss our industrial products yet. We will give credit, and if I am not able to deflate France myself, then the Soviets will help me." Hitler said he had two plans for takeover in Germany: (a) the revolution plan, and (b), the legal takeover plan. The first plan would be a matter of three months, the second plan a matter of three years. Hitler was quoted as saying, "revolution costs five hundred million marks, legal takeover costs two hundred million marks—what will your bankers decide?" After five days a cable from Guaranty Trust arrived for Warburg and is cited in the book as follows:

> *Suggested amounts are out of the question. We don't want to and cannot. Explain to man that such a transfer to Europe will shatter financial market. Absolutely unknown on international territory. Expect long report, before decision is made. Stay there. Continue investigation. Persuade man of impossible demands. Don't forget to include in report own opinion of possibilities for future of man.*

Warburg cabled his report back to New York and three days later received a second cablegram reading:

> *Report received. Prepare to deliver ten, maximum fifteen million dollars. Advise man necessity of aggression against foreign danger.*

The $15 million was accepted for the legal takeover road, not for the revolutionary plan. The money was transferred from Wall Street to Hitler via Warburg as follows—$5 million to be paid at Mendelsohn & Company, Amsterdam; $5 million at the Rotterdamsche Bankvereiniging in Rotterdam; and $5 million at "Banca Italiana."

Warburg travelled to each of these banks, where he reportedly met Heydt, Strasser and Hermann Goering. The groups arranged for checks to be made out to different names in various towns in Germany. In other words, the funds were "laundered" in the modern tradition to disguise their Wall Street origins. In Italy the payment group was reportedly received at the main building of the bank by its president and while waiting in his office two Italian fascists, Rossi and Balbo, were introduced to Warburg, Heydt, Strasser, and Goering. Three days after payment, Warburg returned to New York from Genoa on the *Savoya*. Again, he reported to Carter, Rockefeller, and the other bankers.

The third section of "Financial Sources of National Socialism" is entitled simply "1933." The section records "Sidney Warburg's" third and last meeting with Hitler — on the night the Reichstag was burned. (We noted in Chapter Eight the presence of Roosevelt's friend Putzi Hanfstaengl in the Reichstag.) At this meeting Hitler informed Warburg of Nazi progress towards legal takeover. Since 1931 the Nationalist Socialist party had tripled in size. Massive deposits of weapons had been made near the German border in Belgium, Holland, and Austria — but these weapons required cash payments before delivery. Hitler asked for a minimum of 100 million marks to take care of the final step in the takeover program. Guaranty Trust wired Warburg offering $7 million at most, to be paid as follows — $2 million to the Renania Joint Stock Company in Dusseldorf (the German branch of Royal Dutch), and $5 million to other banks. Warburg reported this offer to Hitler, who requested the $5 million should be sent to the Banca Italiana in Rome and (although the report does not say so) presumably the other $2 million was paid to Dusseldorf. The book concludes with the following statement from Warburg:

> I carried out my assignment strictly down to the last detail. Hitler is dictator of the largest European country. The world has now observed him at work for several months. My opinion of him means nothing now. His actions will prove if he is bad, which I believe he is. For the sake of the German people I hope in my heart that I am wrong. The world continues to suffer under a system that has to bow to a Hitler to keep itself on its feet. Poor world, poor humanity.

This is a synopsis of "Sidney Warburg's" suppressed book on the financial origins of national socialism in Germany. Some of the information in the book is now common knowledge—although only part was generally known in the early 1930s. It is extraordinary to note that the unknown author had access to information that only surfaced many years later—for example, the identity of the von Heydt bank as a Hitler financial conduit. Why was the book taken off the bookstands and suppressed? The stated reason for withdrawal was that "Sidney Warburg" did not exist, that the book was a forgery, and that the Warburg family claimed it contained anti-Semitic and libelous statements.

The information in the book was resurrected after World War II and published in other books in an anti-Semitic context which does not exist in the original 1933 book. Two of these post-war books were Rene Sonderegger's *Spanischer Sommer* and Werner Zimmerman's *Liebet Eure Feinde*.

Most importantly James P. Warburg of New York signed an affidavit in 1949, which was published as an appendix in von Papen's *Memoirs*. This Warburg affidavit emphatically denied the authenticity of the "Sidney Warburg" book and claimed it was a hoax. Unfortunately, James P. Warburg focuses on the 1947 Sonderegger anti-Semitic book *Spanischer Sommer*, not the original suppressed "Sidney Warburg" book published in 1933—where the only anti-Semitism stems from Hitler's alleged statements.

In other words, the Warburg affidavit raised far more questions than it resolved. We should therefore look at Warburg's 1949 affidavit denying the authenticity of *Financial Sources of National Socialism*.

James Paul Warburg's Affidavit

In 1953 Nazi Franz von Papen published his *Memoirs*.[8] This was the same Franz von Papen who had been active in the United States on behalf of German espionage in World War I. In his *Memoirs*, Franz von Papen discusses the question of financing Hitler and places the blame squarely on industrialist Fritz Thyssen and banker Kurt von Schröder. Papen denies that he (Papen) financed Hitler, and indeed no credible evidence has been forthcoming to link von Papen with Hitler's funds (although Zimmerman in *Liebert Eure Feinde* accuses Papen of donating 14 million marks). In this context von Papen mentions "Sidney Warburg's" *The Financial Sources of National Socialism*, together with the two more recent post-World War II books by Werner Zimmerman and Rene Sonderegger (alias Severin Reinhardt).[9] Papen adds that:

> *James P. Warburg is able to refute the whole falsification in his affidavit. . . . For my own part I am most grateful to Mr. Warburg for disposing once and for all of this malicious libel. It is almost impossible to refute accusations of this sort by simple negation, and his authoritative denial has enabled me to give body to my own protestations.*[10]

There are two sections to Appendix II of Papen's book. First is a statement by James P. Warburg; second is the affidavit, dated July 15, 1949.

The opening paragraph of the statement records that in 1933 the Dutch publishing house of Holkema and Warendorf published *De Geldbronnen van Het Nationaal-Socialisme-Drie Gesprekken Met Hitler*, and adds that,

This book was allegedly written by "Sidney Warburg." A partner in the Amsterdam firm of Warburg & Co. informed James P. Warburg of the book and Holkema and Warendorf were informed that no such person as "Sidney Warburg" existed. They thereupon withdrew the book from circulation.

James Warburg then makes two sequential and seemingly contradictory statements:

. . . the book contained a mass of libelous material against various members of my family and against a number of prominent banking houses and individuals in New York. I have never to this day seen a copy of the book. Apparently only a handful of copies escaped the publisher's withdrawal.

Now on the one hand Warburg claims he has never seen a copy of the "Sidney Warburg" book, and on the other hand says it is "libelous" and proceeds to construct a detailed affidavit on a sentence by sentence basis to refute the information supposedly in a book he claims not to have seen! It is very difficult to accept the validity of Warburg's claim he has "never to this day seen a copy of the book." Or if indeed he had not, then the affidavit is worthless.

James Warburg adds that the "Sidney Warburg" book is "obvious anti-Semitism," and the thrust of Warburg's statement is that the "Sidney Warburg" story is pure anti-Semitic propaganda. In fact (and Warburg would have discovered this fact if he had read the book), the *only* anti-Semitic statements in the 1933 book are those attributed to Adolf Hitler, whose anti-Semitic feelings are hardly any great discovery. Apart from Hitler's ravings there is nothing in the original "Sidney Warburg" book remotely connected with anti-Semitism, unless we classify Rockefeller, Glean, Carter, McBean, *etc.* as Jewish. *In fact, it is notable that not a single Jewish banker is named in the book—except for the mythical "Sidney Warburg" who is a courier, not one of the alleged money givers.* Yet we know from an authentic source (Ambassador Dodd) that the Jewish banker Eberhard von Oppenheim did indeed give 200,000 marks to Hitler,[11] and it is unlikely "Sidney Warburg" would have missed this observation if he was deliberately purveying false anti-Semitic propaganda.

The first page of James Warburg's statement concerns the 1933 book. After the first page James Warburg introduces Rene Sonderegger and another book written in 1947. Careful analysis of Warburg's statement and affidavit point up that his denials and assertions essentially refer to Sonderegger and *not* to Sidney Warburg. Now Sonderegger was anti-Semitic and probably was part of a neo-Nazi movement after World War II, but this claim of anti-Semitism cannot be laid to the 1933 book—and that is the crux of the question at issue. In brief, James Paul Warburg starts out by claiming to discuss a book he has never seen but knows to be libelous and anti-Semitic, then without warning shifts the accusation to another book which was certainly anti-Semitic but was published a decade later. Thus, the Warburg affidavit so thoroughly confuses the two books that the reader is lead to condemn the mythical "Sidney Warburg" along with Sonderegger.[12] Let us look at some of J.P. Warburg's statements:

James P. Warburg's Sworn Affidavit New York City, July 15, 1949	Author's Comments on James P. Warburg Affidavit
1. Concerning the wholly false and malicious allegations made by Rene Sonderegger of Zurich, Switzerland, *et al.*, as set forth in the foregoing part of this statement, I, James Paul Warburg, of Greenwich, Connecticut, U.S.A., depose as follows:	Note that the affidavit concerns Rene Sonderegger, *not* the book published by J.G. Shoup in 1933.
2. No such person as "Sidney Warburg" existed in New York City in 1933, nor elsewhere, as far as I know, then or at any other time.	We can assume that the name "Sidney Warburg" is a pseudonym, or used falsely.
3. I never gave any manuscript, diary, notes, cables, or any other documents to any person for translation and publication in Holland, and, specifically, I never gave any such documents to the alleged J.G. Shoup of Antwerp. To the best of my knowledge and recollection I never at any time met any such person.	The affidavit confines itself to grant of materials "for translation and publication in Holland."

4. The telephone conversation between Roger Baldwin and myself, reported by Sonderegger, never took place at all and is pure invention.

Reported by Sonderegger, not "Sidney Warburg."

5. I did not go to Germany at the request of the President of the Guaranty Trust Company in 1929, or at any other time.

But Warburg *did* go to Germany in 1929 and 1930 for the International Acceptance Bank, Inc.

6. I did go to Germany on business for my own bank, The International Acceptance Bank Inc., of New York, in both 1929 and 1930. On neither of these occasions did I have anything to do with investigating the possible prevention of a Communist revolution in Germany by the promotion of a Nazi counter-revolution. As a matter of recorded fact, my opinion at the time was that there was relatively little danger of a Communist revolution in Germany and a considerable danger of a Nazi seizure of power. I am in a position to prove that, on my return from Germany after the Reichstag elections of 1930, I warned my associates that Hitler would very likely come to power in Germany and that the result would be either a Nazi-dominated Europe or a second world war—perhaps both. This can be corroborated as well as the fact that, as a consequence of my warning, my bank proceeded to reduce its German commitments as rapidly as possible.

Note that Warburg, by his own statement, told his banking associates that Hitler would come to power. This claim was made *in 1930*—and the Warburgs continued as *directors* with I.G. Farben and other pro-Nazi firms.

7. I had no discussions anywhere, at any time, with

There is no evidence to contradict this statement.

Hitler, with any Nazi officials, or with anyone else about providing funds for the Nazi Party. Specifically, I had no dealing of this sort with Mendelssohn & Co., or the Rotterdamsche Bankvereiniging or the Banca Italiana. (The latter is probably meant to read Banca d'Italia, with which I likewise had no such dealings.)

So far as can be traced Warburgs were not connected with these banking firms except that the Italian correspondent of Warburg's Bank of Manhattan was "Banca Commerciale Italiana" —which is close to "Banca Italiana."

8. In February 1933 (see pages 191 and 192 of *Spanischer Sommer*) when I am alleged to have brought Hitler the last installment of American funds and to have been received by Goering and Goebbels as well as by Hitler himself, I can prove that I was not in Germany at all. I never set foot in Germany after the Nazis had come to power in January 1933. In January and February I was in New York and Washington, working both with my bank and with President-elect Roosevelt on the then-acute banking crisis. After Mr. Roosevelt's inauguration, on March 3, 1933, I was working with him continuously helping to prepare the agenda for the World Economic Conference, to which I was sent as Financial Adviser in early June. This is a matter of public record.

There is no evidence to contradict these statements. "Sidney Warburg" provides no supporting evidence for his claims.

See *Wall Street and FDR*, (New York: Arlington House Publishers, 1975), for details of FDR's German associations.

10. The foregoing statements should suffice to demonstrate that the whole "Sidney Warburg" myth and the subsequent spurious identification of myself with the non-existent "Sidney" are fabrications of malicious falsehood without the slightest foundation in truth.

No. James P. Warburg states he has never seen the original "Sidney Warburg" book published in Holland in 1933. Therefore his affidavit only applies to the Sonderegger book which *is* inaccurate. Sidney Warburg may well be a myth, but the association of Max Warburg and Paul Warburg with I.G. Farben and Hitler is *not* a myth.

Does James Warburg intend to mislead?

It is true that "Sidney Warburg" may well have been an invention, in the sense that "Sidney Warburg" never existed. We *assume* the name is a fake; but *someone* wrote the book. Zimmerman and Sonderegger may or may not have committed libel to the Warburg name, but unfortunately when we examine James P. Warburg's affidavit as published in von Papen's *Memoirs* we are left as much in the dark as ever. There are three important and unanswered questions: (1) why would James P. Warburg claim as a forgery a book he has not read; (2) why does Warburg's affidavit avoid the key question and divert discussion away from "Sidney Warburg" to the anti-Semitic Sonderegger book published in 1947; and (3) why would James P. Warburg be so insensitive to Jewish suffering in World War II to publish his affidavit in the *Memoirs* of Franz von Papen, who was a prominent Nazi at the heart of the Hitler movement since the early days of 1933?

Not only were the German Warburgs persecuted by Hitler in 1938, but millions of Jews lost their lives to Nazi barbarism. It seems elementary that anyone who has suffered and was sensitive to the past sufferings of German Jews would avoid Nazis, Naziism, and neo-Nazi books like the plague. Yet here we have Nazi von Papen acting as a genial literary host to self-described anti-Nazi James P. Warburg, who apparently welcomes the opportunity. Moreover, the Warburgs had ample opportunity to release such an affidavit with wide publicity without utilizing neo-Nazi channels.

The reader will profit from pondering this situation. The only logical explanation is that some of the facts in the "Sidney Warburg" book are either true, come close to the truth, or are embarrassing to James P. Warburg. One cannot say that Warburg *intends* to mislead (although this might seem an obvious conclusion), because businessmen are notoriously illogical writers and reasoners, and there is certainly nothing to exempt Warburg from this categorization.

Some Conclusions from the "Sidney Warburg" Story

"Sidney Warburg" never existed; in this sense the original 1933 book is a work of fiction. However, many of the then-little-known facts recorded in the book are   curate; and the James Warburg affidavit is not aimed at the original boo   but rather at an anti-Semitic book circulated over a decade later.

Paul Warburg was a director of American I.G. Farben and thus connected with the financing of Hitler. Max Warburg, a director of German I.G. Farben, signed—along with Hitler himself—the document which appointed Hjalmar Schacht to the Reichsbank. These verifiable connections between the Warburgs and Hitler suggest the "Sidney Warburg" story cannot be abandoned as a total forgery without close examination.

Who wrote the 1933 book, and why? I.G. Shoup says the notes were written by a Warburg in England and given to him to translate. The Warburg motive was alleged to be genuine remorse at the amoral behavior of Warburgs and their Wall Street associates. Does this sound like a plausible motive? It has not gone unnoticed that those same Wall Streeters who plot war and revolution are often in their private lives genuinely decent citizens; it is not beyond the realm of reason that one of them had a change of heart or a heavy conscience. But this is not proven.

If the book was a forgery, then by whom was it written? James Warburg admits he does not know the answer, and he writes: "The original purpose of the forgery remains somewhat obscure even today."[13]

Would any government forge the document? Certainly not the British or U.S. governments, which are both indirectly implicated by the book. Certainly not the Nazi government in Germany, although James Warburg appears to suggest this unlikely possibility. Could it be France, or the Soviet Union, or perhaps Austria? France, possibly because France feared the rise of Nazi Germany. Austria is a similar possibility. The Soviet Union is a possibility because the Soviets also had much to fear from Hitler. So it is plausible that France, Austria, or the Soviet Union had some hand in the preparation of the book.

Any private citizen who forged such a book without inside government materials would have to be remarkably well informed. Guaranty Trust is not a particularly well-known bank outside New York, yet there is an extraordinary degree of plausibility about the involvement of Guaranty Trust, because it was the Morgan vehicle used for financing and infiltrating the Bolshevik revolution.[14] Whoever named Guaranty Trust as the vehicle for funding Hitler either knew a great deal more than the man in the street, or had authentic government information.

What would be the motive behind such a book?

The only motive that seems acceptable is that the unknown author had knowledge a war was in preparation and hoped for a public reaction against the Wall Street fanatics and their industrialist friends in Germany—before it was too late. Clearly, *whoever* wrote the book, his motive almost certainly was to warn against Hitlerian aggression and to point to its Wall Street source, because the technical assistance of American companies controlled by Wall Street was still needed to build Hitler's war machine. The Standard Oil hydrogenation patents and financing for the oil from coal plants, the bomb sights, and the other necessary technology had not been fully transferred when the "Sidney Warburg" book was written. Consequently, this could have been a book designed to break the back of Hitler's supporters abroad, to inhibit the planned transfer of U.S. war-making potential, and to eliminate financial and diplomatic support of the Nazi state. If this was the goal, it is regrettable that the book failed to achieve any of these purposes.

CHAPTER ELEVEN

Wall Street-Nazi Collaboration in World War II

Behind the battle fronts in World War II, through intermediaries in Switzerland and North Africa, the New York financial elite collaborated with the Nazi regime. Captured files after the war yielded a mass of evidence demonstrating that for some elements of Big Business, the period 1941-5 was "business as usual." For instance, correspondence between U.S. firms and their French subsidiaries reveals the aid given to the Axis military machine — while the United States was at war with Germany and Italy. Letters between Ford of France and Ford of the U.S. between 1940 and July 1942 were analyzed by the Foreign Funds Control section of the Treasury Department. Their initial report concluded that until mid-1942:

> (1) the business of the Ford subsidiaries in France sub-
> stantially increased; (2) their production was solely for the
> benefit of the Germans and the countries under its occupation;
> (3) the Germans have "shown clearly their wish to protect the
> Ford interests" because of the attitude of strict neutrality
> maintained by Henry Ford and the late Edsel Ford; and (4) the
> increased activity of the French Ford subsidiaries on behalf of
> the Germans received the commendation of the Ford family in
> America.[1]

Similarly, the Rockefeller Chase Bank was accused of collaborating with the Nazis in World War II France, while Nelson Rockefeller had a soft job in Washington D.C.:

> Substantially the same pattern of behavior was pursued by
> the Paris office of the Chase Bank during German occupation.
> An examination of the correspondence between Chase, New

*York, and Chase, France, from the date of the fall of France to
May, 1942 discloses that: (1) the manager of the Paris office
appeased and collaborated with the Germans to place the Chase
banks in a "privileged position;" (2) the Germans held the
Chase Bank in a very special esteem — owing to the international activities of our (Chase) head office and the pleasant
relations which the Paris branch has been maintaining
with many of their (German) banks and their (German) local
organizations and higher officers; (3) the Paris manager was
"very vigorous in enforcing restrictions against Jewish property,
even going so far as to refuse to release funds belonging to Jews
in anticipation that a decree with retroactive provisions prohibiting such release might be published in the near future by the
occupying authorities;" (4) the New York office despite the
above information took no direct steps to remove the undesirable
manager from the Paris office since it "might react against our
(Chase) interests as we are dealing, not with a theory but with a
situation."²*

An official report to then-Secretary of the Treasury Morgenthau concluded that:

*These two situations [i.e., Ford and Chase Bank] convince
us that it is imperative to investigate immediately on the spot the
activities of subsidiaries of at least some of the larger American
firms which were operating in France during German occupation . . . .³*

Treasury officials urged that an investigation be started with the
French subsidiaries of several American banks — that is, Chase, Morgan,
National City, Guaranty, Bankers Trust, and American Express. Although
Chase and Morgan were the only two banks to maintain French offices
throughout the Nazi occupation, in September 1944 all the major New
York banks were pressing the U.S. Government for permission to re-open
pre-war branches. Subsequent Treasury investigation produced documentary evidence of collaboration between both Chase Bank and J.P. Morgan
with the Nazis in World War II. The recommendation for a full investigation is cited in full as follows:

TREASURY DEPARTMENT
INTER-OFFICE COMMUNICATION

Date: December 20, 1944
To: Secretary Morgenthau
From: Mr. Saxon

Examination of the records of the Chase Bank, Paris, and of Morgan and Company, France, have progressed only far enough to permit tentative conclusions and the revelation of a few interesting facts:

CHASE BANK, PARIS

a. Niederman, of Swiss nationality, manager of Chase, Paris, was unquestionably a collaborator;

b. The Chase Head Office in New York was informed of Niederman's collaborationist policy but took no steps to remove him. Indeed there is ample evidence to show that the Head Office in New York viewed Niederman's good relations with the Germans as an excellent means of preserving, unimpaired, the position of the Chase Bank in France;

c. The German authorities were anxious to keep the Chase open and indeed took exceptional measures to provide sources of revenue;

d. The German authorities desired "to be friends" with the important American banks because they expected that these banks would be useful after the war as an instrument of German policy in the United States;

e. The Chase, Paris showed itself most anxious to please the German authorities in every possible way. For example, the Chase zealously maintained the account of the German Embassy in Paris, "as every little thing helps" (to maintain the excellent relations between Chase and the German authorities);

f. The whole objective of the Chase policy and operation was to maintain the position of the bank at any cost.

MORGAN AND COMPANY, FRANCE

a. Morgan and Company regarded itself as a French bank, and therefore obligated to observe French banking laws and regulations, whether Nazi-inspired or not; and did actually do so;

b. Morgan and Company was most anxious to preserve the continuity of its house in France, and, in order to achieve this security, worked out a modus vivendi with the German authorities;

c. Morgan and Company had tremendous prestige with the German authorities, and the Germans boasted of the splendid cooperation of Morgan and Company;

d. Morgan continued its prewar relations with the great French industrial and commercial concerns which were working for Germany, including the Renault Works, since confiscated by the French Government, Puegeqt [sic], Citroen, and many others.

e. The power of Morgan and Company in France bears no relation to the small financial resources of the firm, and the enquiry now in progress will be of real value in allowing us for the first time to study the Morgan pattern in Europe and the manner in which Morgan has used its great power;

f. Morgan and Company constantly sought its ends by playing one government against another in the coldest and most unscrupulous manner.

Mr. Jefferson Caffery, U.S. Ambassador to France, has been kept informed of the progress of this investigation and at all times gave me full support and encouragement, in principle and in fact. Indeed, it was Mr. Caffery himself who asked me how the Ford and General Motors subsidiaries in France had acted during the occupation, and expressed the desire that we should look into these companies after the bank investigation was completed.

RECOMMENDATION

I recommend that this investigation, which, for unavoidable reasons, has progressed slowly up to this time, should now be pressed urgently and that additional needed personnel be sent to Paris as soon as possible.[4]

The full investigation was never undertaken, and no investigation has been made of this presumably treasonable activity down to the present day.

American I.G. in World War II

Collaboration between American businessmen and Nazis in Axis Europe was paralleled by protection of Nazi interests in the United States. In 1939 American I.G. was renamed General Aniline & Film, with General Dyestuffs acting as its exclusive sales agent in the U.S. These names effectively disguised the fact that American I.G. (or General Aniline & Film) was an important producer of major war materials, including atabrine, magnesium, and synthetic rubber. Restrictive agreements with its German parent I.G. Farben reduced American supplies of these military products during World War II.

An American citizen, Halbach, became president of General Dyestuffs in 1930 and acquired majority control in 1939 from Dietrich A. Schmitz, a director of American I.G. and brother of Hermann Schmitz, director of I.G. Farben in Germany and chairman of the board of American I.G. until the outbreak of war in 1939. After Pearl Harbor, the U.S. Treasury blocked Halbach's bank accounts. In June 1942 the Alien Property Custodian seized Halbach's stock in General Dyestuffs and took over the firm as an enemy corporation under the Trading with the Enemy Act. Subsequently, the Alien Property Custodian appointed a new board of directors to act as trustee for the duration of the war. These actions were reasonable and usual practice, but when we probe under the surface another and quite abnormal story emerges.

Between 1942 and 1945 Halbach was nominally a consultant to General Dyestuffs. In fact Halbach ran the company, at $82,000 per year. Louis Johnson, former Assistant Secretary of War, was appointed president of General Dyestuffs by the U.S. Government, for which he received $75,000 a year. Louis Johnson attempted to bring pressure to bear on the U.S. Treasury to unblock Halbach's blocked funds and allow Halbach to develop policies contrary to the interests of the U.S., then at war with Germany. The argument used to get Halbach's bank accounts unblocked was that Halbach was running the company and that the Government-appointed board of directors "would have been lost without Mr. Halbach's knowledge."

During the war Halbach filed suit against the Alien Property Custodian, through the Establishment law firm of Sullivan and Cromwell, to oust the U.S. Government from its control of I.G. Farben companies. These suits were unsuccessful, but Halbach *was* successful in keeping the Farben cartel agreements intact throughout World War II; the Alien Property Custodian never did go into court during World War II on the pending anti-trust suits. Why not? Leo T. Crowley, head of the Alien Property Custodian's office, had John Foster Dulles as his advisor, and John Foster Dulles was a partner in the above-mentioned Sullivan and Cromwell firm, which was acting on behalf of Halbach in its suit against the Alien Property Custodian.

There were other conflict of interest situations we should note. Leo T. Crowley, the Alien Property Custodian, appointed Victor Emanuel to the boards of both General Aniline & Film and General Dyestuffs. Before the war Victor Emanuel was director of the J. Schroder Banking Corporation. Schröder, as we have already seen, was a prominent financier of Hitler and the Nazi party — *and at that very time was a member of Himmler's Circle of Friends, making substantial contributions to S.S. organizations in Germany.*

In turn Victor Emanuel appointed Leo Crowley head of Standard Gas & Electric (controlled by Emanuel) at $75,000 per annum. This sum was in addition to Crowley's salary from the Alien Property Custodian and $10,000 a year as head of the U.S. Government Federal Deposit Insurance Corporation. By 1943 James E. Markham had replaced Crowley as A.P.C. and was also appointed by Emanuel as a director of Standard Gas at $4,-850 per year, in addition to the $10,000 he drew as Alien Property Custodian.

The wartime influence of General Dyestuffs and this cozy government-business coterie on behalf of I.G. Farben is exemplified in the case of American Cyanamid. Before the war I.G. Farben controlled the drug, chemical, and dyestuffs industries in Mexico. During World War II it was proposed to Washington that American Cyanamid take over this Mexican industry and develop an "independent" chemical industry with the old I.G. Farben firms seized by the Mexican Alien Property Custodian.

As hired hands of Schroder banker Victor Emanuel, Crowley and Markham, who were also employees of the U.S. Government, attempted to deal with the question of these I.G. Farben interests in the United States and Mexico. On April 13, 1943 James Markham sent a letter to Secretary of State Cordell Hull objecting to the proposed Cyanamid deal on the grounds it was contrary to the Atlantic Charter and would interfere with the aim of establishing independent firms in Latin America. The Markham position was supported by Henry A. Wallace and Attorney General Francis Biddle.

The forces aligned against the Cyanamid deal were Sterling Drug, Inc. and Winthrop. Both Sterling and Winthrop stood to lose their drug market in Mexico if the Cyanamid deal went through. Also hostile to the Cyanamid deal of course was I.G. Farben's General Aniline and General Dyestuffs, dominated by Victor Emanuel, banker Schröder's former associate.

On the other hand, the State Department and the Office of the Coordinator of Inter-American affairs — which happened to be Nelson Rockefeller's wartime baby — *supported* the proposed Cyanamid deal. The Rockefellers are, of course, also interested in the drug and chemical industries in Latin America. In brief, an American monopoly under influence of Rockefeller would have replaced a Nazi I.G. Farben monopoly.

I.G. Farben won this round in Washington, but more ominous questions are raised when we look at the bombing of Germany in wartime by the U.S.A.A.F. It has long been rumored, but never proven, that Farben received favored treatment — *i.e.*, that it was not bombed. James Stewart Martin comments as follows on favored treatment received by I.G. Farben in the bombing of Germany:

> *Shortly after the armies reached the Rhine at Cologne, we were driving along the west bank within sight of the undamaged I.G. Farben plant at Leverkusen across the river. Without knowing anything about me or my business he (the jeep driver) began to give me a lecture about I.G. Farben and to point at the contrast between the bombed-out city of Cologne and the trio of untouched plants on the fringe: the Ford works and the United Rayon works on the west bank, and the Farben works on the east bank.*[5]

While this accusation is very much of an open question, requiring a great deal of skilled research into the U.S.A.A.F. bombing records, other aspects of favoritism for the Nazis are well recorded.

At the end of World War II, Wall Street moved into Germany through the Control Council to protect their old cartel friends and limit the extent to which the denazification fervor would damage old business relationships. General Lucius Clay, the deputy military governor for Germany, appointed businessmen who opposed denazification to positions of control over the denazification proceeds. *William H. Draper of Dillon, Read, the firm which financed the German cartels back in the 1920s, became General Clay's deputy.*

Banker William Draper, as Brigadier General William Draper, put his control team together from businessmen who had represented American business in pre-war Germany. The General Motors representation included Louis Douglas, a former director of G.M., and Edward S. Zdunke, a pre-war head of General Motors in Antwerp, appointed to supervise the Engineering Section of the Control Council. Peter Hoglund, an expert on German auto industry, was given leave from General Motors. The personnel selection for the Council was undertaken by Colonel Graeme K. Howard — former G.M. representative in Germany and author of a book which "praises totalitarian practices [and] justifies German aggression. . . ."[6]

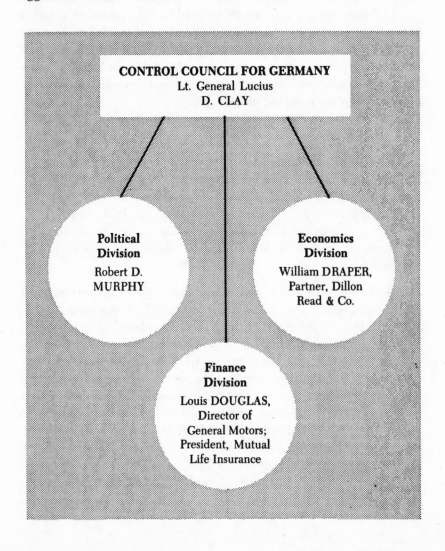

CONTROL COUNCIL FOR GERMANY
Lt. General Lucius
D. CLAY

Political Division
Robert D. MURPHY

Economics Division
William DRAPER, Partner, Dillon Read & Co.

Finance Division
Louis DOUGLAS, Director of General Motors; President, Mutual Life Insurance

Treasury Secretary Morgenthau was deeply disturbed at the implications of this Wall Street monopoly of the fate of Nazi Germany and prepared a memorandum to present to President Roosevelt. The complete Morgenthau memorandum, dated May 29, 1945, reads as follows:

MEMORANDUM

May 29, 1945

Lieutenant-General Lucius D. Clay, as Deputy to General Eisenhower, actively runs the American element of the Control Council for Germany. General Clay's three principal advisers on the Control Council staff are:

1. Ambassador Robert D. Murphy, who is in charge of the Political Division.

2. Louis Douglas, whom General Clay describes ' as my personal adviser on economical, financial and governmental matters." Douglas resigned as Director of the Budget in 1934; and for the following eight years he attacked the government's fiscal policies. Since 1940, Douglas has been president of the Mutual Life Insurance Company, and since December 1944, *he has been a director of the General Motors Corporation.*

3. Brigadier-General William Draper, who is the director of the Economics Division of the Control Council. General Draper is a partner of the banking firm of Dillon, Read and Company.

Sunday's *New York Times* contained the announcement of key personnel who have been appointed by General Clay and General Draper to the Economic Division of the Control Council. The appointments include the following:

1. R.J. Wysor is to be in charge of the metallurgical matters. Wysor was president of the Republic Steel Corporation from 1937 until a recent date, and prior thereto, he was associated with the Bethlehem Steel, Jones and Laughlin Steel Corporation and the Republic Steel Corporation.

2. Edward X. Zdunke is to supervise the engineering section. Prior to the war, Mr. Zdunke was head of General Motors at Antwerp.

3. Philip Gaethke is to be in charge of mining operations. Gaethke was formerly connected with Anaconda Copper and was manager of its smelters and mines in Upper Silesia before the war.

4. Philip P. Clover is to be in charge of handling oil matters. He was formerly a representative of the Socony Vacuum Oil Company in Germany.

5. Peter Hoglund is to deal with industrial production problems. Hoglund is on leave from General Motors and is said to be an expert on German production.

6. Calvin B. Hoover is to be in charge of the Intelligence Group on the Control Council and is also to be a special advisor to General Draper. In a letter to the Editor of the *New York Times* on October 9, 1944, Hoover wrote as follows:

> The publication of Secretary Morgenthau's plan for dealing with Germany has disturbed me deeply . . . such a Carthaginian peace would leave a legacy of hate to poison international relations for generations to come . . . the void in the economy of Europe which would exist through the destruction of all German industry is something which is difficult to contemplate.

7. Laird Bell is to be Chief Counsel of the Economic Division. He is a well-known Chicago lawyer and in May 1944, was elected the president of the *Chicago Daily News*, after the death of Frank Knox.

One of the men who helped General Draper in the selection of personnel for the Economics Division was Colonel Graeme Howard, a vice-president of General Motors, who was in charge of their overseas business and who was a leading representative of General Motors in Germany prior to the war. Howard is the author of a book in which he praises totalitarian practices, justifies German aggression and the Munich policy of appeasement, and blames Roosevelt for precipitating the war.

So when we examine the Control Council for Germany under General Lucius D. Clay we find that the head of the finance division was Louis Douglas, director of the Morgan-controlled General Motors and president of Mutual Life Insurance. (Opel, the General Motors German subsidiary, had been Hitler's biggest tank producer.) The head of the Control Council's Economics Division was William Draper, a partner in the Dillon, Read firm that had so much to do with building Nazi Germany in the first place. All three men were, not surprisingly in the light of more recent findings, members of the Council on Foreign Relations.

Were American Industrialists and Financiers Guilty of War Crimes?

The Nuremburg War Crimes Trials proposed to select those responsible for World War II preparations and atrocities and place them on trial. Whether such a procedure is morally justifiable is a debatable matter; there is some justification for holding that Nuremburg was a political farce far removed from legal principle.[7] However, if we assume that there *is* such legal and moral justification, then surely any such trial should apply to *all*, irrespective of nationality. What for example should exempt Franklin D. Roosevelt and Winston Churchill, but not exempt Adolf Hitler and Goering? If the offense is preparation for war, and not blind vengeance, then justice should be impartial.

The directives prepared by the U.S. Control Council in Germany for the arrest and detention of war criminals refers to "Nazis" and "Nazi sympathizers," not "Germans." The relevant extracts are as follows:

> *a. You will search out, arrest, and hold, pending receipt by you of further instructions as to their disposition, Adolph Hitler, his chief Nazi associates, other war criminals and all persons who have participated in planning or carrying out Nazi enterprises involving or resulting in atrocities or war crimes.*

Then follows a list of the categories of persons to be arrested, including:

> *(8) Nazis and Nazi sympathizers holding important and key positions in (a) National and Gau Civic and economic organizations; (b) corporations and other organizations in which the government has a major financial interest; (c) industry, commerce, agriculture, and finance; (d) education; (e) the judiciary; and (f) the press, publishing houses and other agencies disseminating news and propaganda.*

Top American industrialists and financiers named in this book are covered by the categories listed above. Henry Ford and Edsel Ford respectively contributed money to Hitler and profited from German wartime production. Standard Oil of New Jersey, General Electric, General Motors, and I.T.T. certainly made financial or technical contributions which comprise *prima facie* evidence of "participating in planning or carrying out Nazi enterprises."

There is, in brief, evidence which suggests:

(a) cooperation with the Wehrmacht (Ford Motor Company, Chase Bank, Morgan Bank);

(b) aid to the Nazi Four Year Plan and economic mobilization for war (Standard Oil of New Jersey);

(c) creating and equipping the Nazi war machine (I.T.T.);

(d) stockpiling critical materials for the Nazis (Ethyl Corporation);

(e) weakening the Nazis' potential enemies (American I.G. Farben); and,

(f) carrying on of propaganda, intelligence, and espionage (American I.G. Farben and Rockefeller public-relations man Ivy Lee).

At the very least there is sufficient evidence to demand a thorough and impartial investigation. However, as we have noted previously, these same firms and financiers were prominent in the 1933 election of Roosevelt and consequently had sufficient political pull to squelch threats of investigation. Extracts from the Morgenthau diary demonstrate that Wall Street political power was sufficient even to control the appointment of officers responsible for the denazification and eventual government of post-war Germany.

Did these American firms know of their assistance to Hitler's military machine? According to the firms themselves, emphatically not. They claim innocence of any intent to aid Hitler's Germany. Witness a telegram sent by the chairman of the board of Standard Oil of New Jersey to Secretary of War Patterson after World War II, when preliminary investigation of Wall Street assistance was under way:

> *During the entire period of our business contacts, we had no inkling of Farben's conniving part in Hitler's brutal politics. We offer any help we can give to see that complete truth is brought to light, and that rigid justice is done.*
>
> *F.W. Abrams, Chairman of Board*

Unfortunately, the evidence presented is contrary to Abrams' telegraphed assertions. Standard Oil of New Jersey not only aided Hitler's war machine, but had knowledge of this assistance. Emil Helfferich, the board chairman of a Standard of New Jersey subsidiary, was a member of the Keppler Circle *before* Hitler came to power; he continued to give financial contributions to Himmler's Circle as late as 1944.

Accordingly, it is not at all difficult to visualize why Nazi industrialists were puzzled by "investigation" and assumed at the end of the war that their Wall Street friends would bail them out and protect them from the wrath of those who had suffered. These attitudes were presented to the Kilgore Committee in 1946:

> *You might also be interested in knowing, Mr. Chairman, that the top I.G. Farben people and others, when we questioned them about these activities, were inclined at times to be very indignant. Their general attitude and expectation was that the war was over and we ought now to be assisting them in helping to get I.G. Farben and German industry back on its feet. Some of them have outwardly said that this questioning and investigation was, in their estimation, only a phenomenon of short duration, because as soon as things got a little settled they would expect their friends in the United States and in England to be coming over. Their friends, so they said, would put a stop to activities such as these investigations and would see that they got the treatment which they regarded as proper and that assistance would be given to them to help reestablish their industry.*[8]

CHAPTER TWELVE

Conclusions

We have demonstrated with documentary evidence a number of critical associations between Wall Street international bankers and the rise of Hitler and Naziism in Germany.

First: that Wall Street financed the German cartels in the mid-1920s which in turn proceeded to bring Hitler to power.

Second: that the financing for Hitler and his S.S. street thugs came in part from affiliates or subsidiaries of U.S. firms, including Henry Ford in 1922, payments by I.G. Farben and General Electric in 1933, followed by the Standard Oil of New Jersey and I.T.T. subsidiary payments to Heinrich Himmler up to 1944.

Third: that U.S. multi-nationals under the control of Wall Street profited handsomely from Hitler's military construction program in the 1930s and at least until 1942.

Fourth: that these same international bankers used political influence in the U.S. to cover up their wartime collaboration and to do this infiltrated the U.S. Control Commission for Germany.

Our evidence for these four major assertions can be summarized as follows:

In Chapter One we presented evidence that the Dawes and Young Plans for German reparations were formulated by Wall Streeters, temporarily wearing the hats of statesmen, and these loans generated a rain of profits for these international bankers. Owen Young of General Electric, Hjalmar Schacht, A. Voegler, and others intimately connected with Hitler's accession to power had earlier been the negotiators for the U.S. and German sides, respectively. Three Wall Street houses — Dillon, Read; Harris, Forbes; and, National City Company — handled three-quarters of the reparations loans used to create the German cartel system, including the dominant I.G. Farben and Vereinigte Stahlwerke, which together produced 95 percent of the explosives for the Nazi side in World War II.

The central role of I.G. Farben in Hitler's *coup d'état* was reviewed in

Chapter Two. The directors of American I.G. (Farben) were identified as prominent American businessmen: Walter Teagle, a close Roosevelt associate and backer and an NRA administrator; banker Paul Warburg (his brother Max Warburg was on the board of I.G. Farben in Germany); and Edsel Ford. Farben contributed 400,000 RM directly to Schacht and Hess for use in the crucial 1933 elections and Farben was subsequently in the forefront of military development in Nazi Germany.

A donation of 60,000 RM was made to Hitler by German General Electric (A.E.G.), which had four directors and a 25-30 percent interest held by the U.S. General Electric parent company. This role was described in Chapter Three, and we found that Gerard Swope, an originator of Roosevelt's New Deal (its National Recovery Administration segment), together with Owen Young of the Federal Reserve Bank of New York and Clark Minor of International General Electric, were the dominant Wall Streeters in A.E.G. and the most significant single influence.

We also found no evidence to indict the German electrical firm Siemens, which was *not* under Wall Street control. In contrast, there is documentary evidence that both A.E.G. and Osram, the other units of the German electrical industry — both of which had U.S. participation and control — *did* finance Hitler. In fact, almost all directors of German General Electric were Hitler backers, either directly through A.E.G. or indirectly through other German firms. G.E. rounded out its Hitler support by technical cooperation with Krupp, aimed at restricting U.S. development of tungsten carbide, which worked to the detriment of the U.S. in World War II. We concluded that A.E.G. plants in Germany managed, by a yet unknown maneuver, to avoid bombing by the Allies.

An examination of the role of Standard Oil of New Jersey (which was and is controlled by the Rockefeller interests) was undertaken in Chapter Four. Standard Oil apparently did not finance Hitler's accession to power in 1933 (that part of the "myth of Sidney Warburg" is not proven). On the other hand, payments were made up to 1944 by Standard Oil of New Jersey, to develop synthetic gasoline for war purposes on behalf of the Nazis and, through its wholly owned subsidiary, to Heinrich Himmler's S.S. Circle of Friends for political purposes. Standard Oil's role was technical aid to Nazi development of synthetic rubber and gasoline through a U.S. research company under the management control of Standard Oil. The Ethyl Gasoline Company, jointly owned by Standard Oil of New Jersey and General Motors, was instrumental in supplying vital ethyl lead to Nazi Germany — over the written protests of the U.S. War Department — with the clear knowledge that the ethyl lead was for Nazi military purposes.

In Chapter Five we demonstrated that International Telephone and Telegraph Company, one of the more notorious multi-nationals, worked both sides of World War II through Baron Kurt von Schröder, of the Schroder banking group. I.T.T. also held a 28-percent interest in Focke-Wolfe aircraft, which manufactured excellent German fighter planes. We also found that Texaco (Texas Oil Company) was involved in Nazi endeavors through German attorney Westrick, but dropped its chairman of the board Rieber when these endeavors were publicized.

Henry Ford was an early (1922) Hitler backer and Edsel Ford continued the family tradition in 1942 by encouraging French Ford to profit from arming the German Wehrmacht. Subsequently, these Ford-produced vehicles were used against American soldiers as they landed in France in 1944. For his early recognition of, and timely assistance to, the Nazis, Henry Ford received a Nazi medal in 1938. The records of French Ford suggest Ford Motor received kid glove treatment from the Nazis after 1940.

The provable threads of Hitler financing are drawn together in Chapter Seven and answer with precise names and figures the question, who financed Adolf Hitler? This chapter indicts Wall Street and, incidentally, no one else of consequence in the United States except the Ford family. The Ford family is not normally associated with Wall Street but is certainly a part of the "power elite."

In earlier chapters we cited several Roosevelt associates, including Teagle of Standard Oil, the Warburg family, and Gerard Swope. In Chapter Eight the role of Putzi Hanfstaengl, another Roosevelt friend and a participant in the Reichstag fire, is traced. The composition of the Nazi inner circle during World War II, and the financial contributions of Standard Oil of New Jersey and I.T.T. subsidiaries, are traced in Chapter Nine. Documentary proof of these monetary contributions is presented. Kurt von Schröder is identified as the key intermediary in this S.S. "slush fund."

Finally, in Chapter Ten we reviewed a book suppressed in 1934 and the "myth of 'Sidney Warburg.'" The suppressed book accused the Rockefellers, the Warburgs, and the major oil companies of financing Hitler. While the name "Sidney Warburg" was no doubt an invention, the extraordinary fact remains that the argument in the suppressed "Sidney Warburg" book is remarkably close to the evidence presented now. It also remains a puzzle why James Paul Warburg, fifteen years later, would want to attempt, in a rather transparently slipshod manner, to refute the contents of the "Warburg" book, a book he claims not to have seen. It is perhaps even more of a puzzle why Warburg would choose Nazi von Papen's *Memoirs* as the vehicle to present his refutation.

Finally, in Chapter Eleven we examined the roles of the Morgan and Chase Banks in World War II, specifically their collaboration with the Nazis in France while a major war was raging.

In other words, as in our two previous examinations of the links between New York international bankers and major historical events, we find a provable pattern of subsidy and political manipulation.

The Pervasive Influence of International Bankers

Looking at the broad array of facts presented in the three volumes of the Wall Street series, we find persistent recurrence of the same names: Owen Young, Gerard Swope, Hjalmar Schacht, Bernard Baruch, *etc.*; the same international banks: J. P. Morgan, Guaranty Trust, Chase Bank; and the same location in New York: usually 120 Broadway.

This group of international bankers backed the Bolshevik Revolution and subsequently profited from the establishment of a Soviet Russia. This group backed Roosevelt and profited from New Deal socialism. This group also backed Hitler and certainly profited from German armament in the 1930s. When Big Business should have been running its business operations at Ford Motor, Standard of New Jersey, and so on, we find it actively and deeply involved in political upheavals, war, and revolutions in three major countries.

The version of history presented here is that the financial elite knowingly and with premeditation assisted the Bolshevik Revolution of 1917 in concert with German bankers. After profiting handsomely from the German hyper-inflationary distress of 1923, and planning to place the German reparations burden onto the backs of American investors, Wall Street found it had brought about the 1929 financial crisis.

Two men were then backed as leaders for major Western countries: Franklin D. Roosevelt in the United States and Adolf Hitler in Germany. The Roosevelt New Deal and Hitler's Four Year Plan had great similarities. The Roosevelt and Hitler plans were plans for fascist takeovers of their respective countries. While Roosevelt's NRA failed, due to then-operating constitutional constraints, Hitler's Plan succeeded.

Why did the Wall Street elite, the international bankers, want Roosevelt and Hitler in power? This is an aspect we have not explored. According to the "myth of 'Sidney Warburg,'" Wall Street wanted a policy of revenge; that is, it wanted war in Europe between France and Germany. We know even from Establishment history that both Hitler and Roosevelt acted out policies leading to war.

The link-ups between persons and events in this three-book series would require another book. But a single example will perhaps indicate the remarkable concentration of power within a relatively few organizations, and the use of this power.

On May 1st, 1918, when the Bolsheviks controlled only a small fraction of Russia (and were to come near to losing even that fraction in the summer of 1918), the American League to Aid and Cooperate with Russia was organized in Washington, D.C. to support the Bolsheviks. This was not a "Hands off Russia" type of committee formed by the Communist Party U.S.A. or its allies. It was a committee *created by Wall Street* with George P. Whalen of Vacuum Oil Company as Treasurer and Coffin and Oudin of General Electric, along with Thompson of the Federal Reserve System, Willard of the Baltimore & Ohio Railroad, and assorted socialists.

When we look at the rise of Hitler and Naziism we find Vacuum Oil and General Electric well represented. Ambassador Dodd in Germany was struck by the monetary and technical contribution by the Rockefeller-controlled Vacuum Oil Company in building up military gasoline facilities for the Nazis. The Ambassador tried to warn Roosevelt. Dodd believed, in his apparent naiveté of world affairs, that Roosevelt would intervene, but Roosevelt himself was backed by these same oil interests and Walter Teagle of Standard Oil of New Jersey and the NRA was on the board of Roosevelt's Warm Springs Foundation. So, in but one of many examples, we find the Rockefeller-controlled Vacuum Oil Company prominently assisting in the creation of Bolshevik Russia, the military build-up of Nazi Germany, and backing Roosevelt's New Deal.

Is the United States Ruled by a Dictatorial Elite?

Within the last decade or so, certainly since the 1960s, a steady flow of literature has presented a thesis that the United States is ruled by a self-perpetuating and unelected power elite. Even further, most of these books aver that this elite controls, or at the least heavily influences, all foreign and domestic policy decisions, and that no idea becomes respectable or is published in the United States without the tacit approval, or perhaps lack of disapproval, of this elitist circle.

Obviously the very flow of anti-establishment literature by itself testifies that the United States cannot be wholly under the thumb of any single group or elite. On the other hand, anti-establishment literature is not fully recognized or reasonably discussed in academic or media circles. More often than not it consists of a limited edition, privately produced, almost hand-to-hand circulated. There are *some* exceptions, true; but not enough to dispute the observation that anti-establishment critics do not easily enter normal information/distribution channels.

Whereas in the early and mid-1960s, any concept of rule by a conspiratorial elite, or indeed any kind of elite, was reason enough to dismiss the proponent out of hand as a "nut case," the atmosphere for such concepts has changed radically. The Watergate affair probably added the final touches to a long-developing environment of skepticism and doubt. We are almost at the point where anyone who accepts, for example, the Warren Commission report, or believes that that the decline and fall of Mr. Nixon did not have some conspiratorial aspects, is suspect. In brief, no one any longer really believes the Establishment information process. And there is a wide variety of alternative presentations of events now available for the curious.

Several hundred books, from the full range of the political and philosophical spectrum, add bits and pieces of evidence, more hypotheses, and more accusations. What was not too long ago a kooky idea, talked about at midnight behind closed doors, in hushed and almost conspiratorial whispers, is now openly debated — not, to be sure, in Establishment newspapers but certainly on non-network radio talk shows, the underground press, and even from time to time in books from respectable Establishment publishing houses.

So let us ask the question again: Is there an unelected power elite behind the U.S. Government?

A substantive and often-cited source of information is Carroll Quigley, Professor of International Relations at Georgetown University, who in 1966 had published a monumental modern history entitled *Tragedy and Hope.*[1] Quigley's book is apart from others in this revisionist vein, by virtue of the fact that it was based on a two-year study of the internal documents of one of the power centers. Quigley traces the history of the power elite:

> ... *the powers of financial capitalism had another far reaching aim, nothing less than to create a world system of financial control in private hands able to dominate the political system of each country and the economy of the world as a whole.*

Quigley also demonstrates that the Council on Foreign Relations, the National Planning Association, and other groups are "semi-secret" policy-making bodies under the control of this power elite.

In the following tabular presentation we have listed five such revisionist books, including Quigley's. Their essential theses and compatibility with the three volumes of the "Wall Street" series are summarized. It is surprising that in the three major historical events noted, Carroll Quigley is not at all consistent with the "Wall Street" series evidence. Quigley goes a long way to provide evidence for the *existence* of the power elite, but does not penetrate the *operations* of the elite.

Possibly, the papers used by Quigley had been vetted, and did not include documentation on elitist manipulation of such events as the Bolshevik Revolution, Hitler's accession to power, and the election of Roosevelt in 1933. More likely, these political manipulations may not be recorded at all in the files of the power groups. They may have been unrecorded actions by a small *ad hoc* segment of the elite. It is noteworthy that the documents used by this author came from government sources, recording the day-to-day actions of Trotsky, Lenin, Roosevelt, Hitler, J.P. Morgan and the various firms and banks involved.

On the other hand, such authors as Jules Archer, Gary Allen, Helen P. Lasell, and William Domhoff, writing from widely different political standpoints,[2] *are* consistent with the "Wall Street" evidence. These writers present a hypothesis of a power elite manipulating the U.S. Government. The "Wall Street" series demonstrates how this hypothesized "power elite" has manipulated specific historical events.

Obviously any such exercise of unconstrained and supra-legal power is unconstitutional, even though wrapped in the fabric of law-abiding actions. We can therefore legitimately raise the question of the existence of a subversive force operating to remove constitutionally guaranteed rights.

The New York Elite as a Subversive Force

Twentieth-century history, as recorded in Establishment textbooks

IS THE EVIDENCE IN THE "WALL STREET" SERIES CONSISTENT WITH RELATED REVISIONIST ARGUMENTS PRESENTED ELSEWHERE?

Author and Title:	Essential Thesis:	Is the Thesis Consistent with:		
		(1) *Wall Street and the Bolshevik Revolution*	(2) *Wall Street and FDR*	(3) *Wall Street and the Rise of Hitler*
Carroll QUIGLEY: *Tragedy and Hope* (1)	"Semi-secret" Eastern Establishment and interlocks have dominant role in planning and policy in U.S.	Quigley does not include evidence of Wall Street in the Bolshevik Revolution (pp. 385-9)	No: Quigley's argument is totally inconsistent with above (see p. 533)	Quigley's account of the rise of Hitler (pp. 529-33) does not include evidence of Establishment involvement.
Jules ARCHER: *Plot to Seize the White House* (2)	In 1933-4 there was a Wall Street conspiracy to remove FDR and install a fascist dictatorship in the United States.	Not relevant, but Wall Street elements cited by Archer were involved in the Bolshevik Revolution.	Yes: in general Archer's evidence is consistent, except that the role of FDR is interpreted differently.	Those parts in Archer bearing on Hitler and Naziism are consistent with the above.
Gary ALLEN: *None Dare Call It Conspiracy* (3)	There exists a secret conspiracy (the Council on Foreign Relations) to install a dictatorship in the U.S. and ultimately to control the world.	Yes, except for minor variances on financing.	Not included in Allen but is consistent.	Not included in Allen but is consistent.

Helen P. LASELL: *Power Behind the Government Today* (4)	The Council on Foreign Relations is a secret subversive organization dedicated to the overthrow of Constitutional government in the U.S.	Lasell's evidence is consistent with above.	Lasell's evidence is consistent with above.	Lasell's evidence is consistent with above.
William DOMHOFF: *Who Rules America?* (5)	There is a "power elite" which controls all major banks, corporations, foundations, the executive branch, and the regulatory agencies of the U.S. government.	Above series extends Domhoff's argument to foreign policy.	Above series extends Domhoff's argument to Presidential elections.	Above series extends Domhoff's argument to foreign policy.

1. New York: MacMillan, 1966.
2. New York: Hawthorn, 1973.
3. Seal Beach: Concord Press, 1971.
4. New York: Liberty, 1963.
5. New Jersey: Prentice Hall, 1967.

and journals, is inaccurate. It is a history which is based solely upon those official documents which various Administrations have seen fit to release for public consumption.

But an accurate history cannot be based on a selective release of documentary archives. Accuracy requires access to all documents. In practice, as previously classified documents in the U.S. State Department files, the British Foreign Office, and the German Foreign Ministry archives and other depositories are acquired, a new version of history has emerged; the prevailing Establishment version is seen to be, not only inaccurate, but designed to hide a pervasive fabric of deceit and immoral conduct.

The center of political power, as authorized by the U.S. Constitution, is with an elected Congress and an elected President, working within the framework and under the constraints of a Constitution, as interpreted by an unbiased Supreme Court. We have in the past *assumed* that political power is consequently carefully exercised by the Executive and legislative branch, after due deliberation and assessment of the wishes of the electorate. In fact, nothing could be further from this assumption. The electorate has long suspected, but now knows, that political promises are worth nothing. Lies are the order of the day for policy implementors. Wars are started (and stopped) with no shred of coherent explanation. Political words have never matched political deeds. Why not? Apparently because the center of political power has been elsewhere than with elected and presumably responsive representatives in Washington, and this power elite has its own objectives, which are inconsistent with those of the public at large.

In this three-volume series we have identified for three historical events the seat of political power in the United States — the power behind the scenes, the hidden influence on Washington — as that of the financial establishment in New York: the private international bankers, more specifically the financial houses of J.P. Morgan, the Rockefeller-controlled Chase Manhattan Bank, and in earlier days (before amalgamation of their Manhattan Bank with the former Chase Bank), the Warburgs.

The United States has, in spite of the Constitution and its supposed constraints, become a quasi-totalitarian state. While we do not (yet) have the overt trappings of dictatorship, the concentration camps and the knock on the door at midnight, we most certainly do have threats and actions aimed at the survival of non-Establishment critics, use of the Internal Revenue Service to bring dissidents in line, and manipulation of the

Constitution by a court system that is politically subservient to the Establishment.

It is in the pecuniary interests of the international bankers to centralize political power — and this centralization can best be achieved within a collectivist society, such as socialist Russia, national socialist Germany, or a Fabian socialist United States.

There can be no full understanding and appreciation of twentieth-century American politics and foreign policy without the realization that this financial elite effectively monopolizes Washington policy.

In case after case, newly released documentation implicates this elite and confirms this hypothesis. The revisionist versions of the entry of the United States into World Wars I and II, Korea, and Vietnam reveal the influence and objectives of this elite.

For most of the twentieth century the Federal Reserve System, particularly the Federal Reserve Bank of New York (which is outside the control of Congress, unaudited and uncontrolled, with the power to print money and create credit at will), has exercised a virtual monopoly over the direction of the American economy. In foreign affairs the Council on Foreign Relations, superficially an innocent forum for academics, businessmen, and politicians, contains within its shell, perhaps unknown to many of its members, a power center that unilaterally determines U.S. foreign policy. The major objective of this submerged — and obviously subversive — foreign policy is the acquisition of markets and economic power (*profits*, if you will), for a small group of giant multi-nationals under the virtual control of a few banking investment houses and controlling families.

Through foundations controlled by this elite, research by compliant and spineless academics, "conservatives" as well as "liberals," has been directed into channels useful for the objectives of the elite essentially to maintain this subversive and unconstitutional power apparatus.

Through publishing houses controlled by this same financial elite unwelcome books have been squashed and useful books promoted; fortunately publishing has few barriers to entry and is almost atomistically competitive. Through control of a dozen or so major newspapers, run by editors who think alike, public information can be almost orchestrated at will. Yesterday, the space program; today, an energy crisis or a campaign for ecology; tomorrow, a war in the Middle East or some other manufactured "crisis."

The total result of this manipulation of society by the Establishment elite has been four major wars in sixty years, a crippling national debt, abandonment of the Constitution, suppression of freedom and opportunity, and creation of a vast credibility gulf between the man in the street and Washington, D.C. While the transparent device of two major parties trumpeting artificial differences, circus-like conventions, and the cliché of "bipartisan foreign policy" no longer carries credibility, and the financial elite itself recognizes that its policies lack public acceptance, it is obviously prepared to go it alone without even nominal public support.

In brief, we now have to consider and debate whether this New York-based elitist Establishment is a subversive force operating with deliberation and knowledge to suppress the Constitution and a free society. That will be the task ahead in the next decade.

The Slowly Emerging Revisionist Truth

The arena for this debate and the basis for our charges of subversion is the evidence provided by the revisionist historian. Slowly, over decades, book by book, almost line by line, the truth of recent history has emerged as documents are released, probed, analyzed, and set within a more valid historical framework.

Let us consider a few examples. American entry into World War II was supposedly precipitated, according to the Establishment version, by the Japanese attack on Pearl Harbor. Revisionists have established that Franklin D. Roosevelt and General Marshall *knew* of the impending Japanese attack and did nothing to warn the Pearl Harbor military authorities. The Establishment wanted war with Japan. Subsequently, the Establishment made certain that Congressional investigation of Pearl Harbor would fit the Roosevelt whitewash. In the words of Percy Greaves, chief research expert for the Republican minority on the Joint Congressional Committee investigating Pearl Harbor:

> *The complete facts will never be known. Most of the so-called investigations have been attempts to suppress, mislead, or confuse those who seek the truth. From the beginning to the end, facts and files have been withheld so as to reveal only those items of information which benefit the administration under investigation. Those seeking the truth are told that other facts or documents cannot be revealed because they are intermingled in*

personal diaries, pertain to our relations with foreign countries,
or are sworn to contain no information of value.[3]

But this was not the first attempt to bring the United States into war, or the last. The Morgan interests, in concert with Winston Churchill, tried to bring the U.S. into World War I as early as 1915 and succeeded in doing so in 1917. Colin Thompson's *Lusitania* implicates President Woodrow Wilson in the sinking of the *Lusitania* — a horror device to generate a public backlash to draw the United States into war with Germany. Thompson demonstrates that Woodrow Wilson knew *four days beforehand* that the *Lusitania* was carrying six-million rounds of ammunition plus explosives, and therefore, "passengers who proposed to sail on that vessel were sailing in violation of statute of this country."[5]

The British Board of Inquiry under Lord Mersey was *instructed* by the British Government "that it is considered politically expedient that Captain Turner, the master of the *Lusitania*, be most prominently blamed for the disaster."

In retrospect, given Colin Thompson's evidence, the blame is more fairly to be attributed to President Wilson, "Colonel" House, J. P. Morgan, and Winston Churchill; this conspiratorial elite should have been brought to trial for willful negligence, if not treason. It is to Lord Mersey's eternal credit that after performing his "duty" under instructions from His Majesty's government, and placing the blame on Captain Turner, he resigned, rejected his fee, and from that date on refused to handle British government commissions. To his friends Lord Mersey would only say about the *Lusitania* case that it was a "dirty business."

Then in 1933-4 came the attempt by the Morgan firm to install a fascist dictatorship in the United States. In the words of Jules Archer, it was planned to be a Fascist *putsch* to take over the government and "run it under a dictator on behalf of America's bankers and industrialists."[5] Again, a single courageous individual emerged — General Smedley Darlington Butler, who blew the whistle on the Wall Street conspiracy. And once again Congress stands out, particularly Congressmen Dickstein and MacCormack, by its gutless refusal to do no more than conduct a token whitewash investigation.

Since World War II we have seen the Korean War and the Vietnamese War — meaningless, meandering no-win wars costly in dollars and lives, with no other major purpose but to generate multibillion-dollar armaments contracts. Certainly these wars were not fought to restrain communism, because for fifty years the Establishment has been nurturing and subsidizing the Soviet Union which supplied armaments to the other sides in both wars — Korea and Vietnam. So our revisionist history will show that the United States directly or indirectly armed both sides in at least Korea and Vietnam.

In the assassination of President Kennedy, to take a domestic example, it is difficult to find anyone who today accepts the findings of the Warren Commission — except perhaps the members of that Commission. Yet key evidence is still hidden from public eyes for 50 to 75 years. The Watergate affair demonstrated even to the man in the street that the White House can be a vicious nest of intrigue and deception.

Of all recent history the story of Operation Keelhaul[6] is perhaps the most disgusting. Operation Keelhaul was the forced repatriation of millions of Russians at the orders of President (then General) Dwight D. Eisenhower, in direct violation of the Geneva Convention of 1929 and the long-standing American tradition of political refuge. Operation Keelhaul, which contravenes all our ideas of elementary decency and individual freedom, was undertaken at the direct orders of General Eisenhower and, we may now presume, was a part of a long-range program of nurturing collectivism, whether it be Soviet communism, Hitler's Naziism, or FDR's New Deal. Yet until recent publication of documentary evidence by Julius Epstein, anyone who dared to suggest Eisenhower would betray millions of innocent individuals for political purposes was viciously and mercilessly attacked.[7]

What this revisionist history really teaches us is that our willingness as individual citizens to surrender political power to an elite has cost the world approximately two-hundred-million persons killed from 1820 to 1975. Add to that untold misery the concentration camps, the political prisoners, the suppression and oppression of those who try to bring the truth to light.

When will it all stop? It will not stop until we act upon one simple axiom: that the power system continues only so long as *individuals* want it to continue, and it will continue only so long as *individuals* try to get something for nothing. The day when a majority of individuals declares or acts as if it wants nothing from government, declares it will look after its own welfare and interests, then on *that* day power elites are doomed. The attraction to "go along" with power elites is the attraction of something for nothing. That is the bait. The Establishment always offers something for nothing; but the something is taken from someone else, as taxes or plunder, and awarded elsewhere in exchange for political support.

Periodic crises and wars are used to whip up support for other plunder-reward cycles which in effect tighten the noose around our individual liberties. And of course we have hordes of academic sponges, amoral businessmen, and just plain hangers-on, to act as non-productive recipients for the plunder.

Stop the circle of plunder and immoral reward and elitist structures collapse. But not until a majority finds the moral courage and the internal fortitude to reject the something-for-nothing con game and replace it by voluntary associations, voluntary communes, or local rule and decentralized societies, will the killing and the plunder cease.

APPENDIX A

Program of the National Socialist German Workers Party

Note: This program is important because it demonstrates that the nature of Naziism was known publicly as early as 1920.

THE PROGRAM

The program of the German Workers' Party is limited as to period. The leaders have no intention, once the aims announced in it have been achieved, of setting up fresh ones, merely in order to increase the discontent of the masses artificially, and so ensure the continued existence of the Party.

1. We demand the union of all Germans to form a Great Germany on the basis of the right of the self-determination enjoyed by nations.

2. We demand equality of rights for the German People in its dealings with other nations, and abolition of the Peace Treaties of Versailles and St. Germain.

3. We demand land and territory (colonies) for the nourishment of our people and for settling our superfluous population.

4. None but members of the nation may be citizens of the State. None but those of German blood, whatever their creed, may be members of the nation. No Jew, therefore, may be a member of the nation.

5. Any one who is not a citizen of the State may live in Germany only as a guest and must be regarded as being subject to foreign laws.

6. The right of voting on the State's government and legislation is to be enjoyed by the citizen of the State alone. We demand therefore that all official appointments, of whatever kind, whether in the Reich, in the country, or in the smaller localities, shall be granted to citizens of the State alone.

We oppose the corrupting custom of Parliament of filling posts merely with a view to party considerations, and without reference to character or capability.

7. We demand that the State shall make it its first duty to promote the industry and livelihood of citizens of the State. If it is not possible to nourish the entire population of the State, foreign nationals (non-citizens of the State) must be excluded from the Reich.

8. All non-German immigration must be prevented. We demand that all non-Germans, who entered Germany subsequent to August 2nd, 1914, shall be required forthwith to depart from the Reich.

9. All citizens of the State shall be equal as regards rights and duties.

10. It must be the first duty of each citizen of the State to work with his mind or with his body. The activities of the individual may not clash with the interests of

the whole, but must proceed within the frame of the community and be for the general good.

We demand therefore:

11. Abolition of incomes unearned by work.

ABOLITION OF THE THRALDOM OF INTEREST

12. In view of the enormous sacrifice of life and property demanded of a nation by every war, personal enrichment due to a war must be regarded as a crime against the nation. We demand therefore ruthless confiscation of all war gains.

13. We demand nationalisation of all businesses which have been up to the present formed into companies (Trusts).

14. We demand that the profits from wholesale trade shall be shared out.

15. We demand extensive development of provision for old age.

16. We demand creation and maintenance of a healthy middle class, immediate communalisation of wholesale business premises, and their lease at a cheap rate to small traders, and that extreme consideration shall be shown to all small purveyors to the State, district authorities and smaller localities.

17. We demand land-reform suitable to our national requirements, passing of a law for confiscation without compensation of land for communal purposes; abolition of interest on land loans, and prevention of all speculation in land.

18. We demand ruthless prosecution of those whose activities are injurious to the common interest. Sordid criminals against the nation, usurers, profiteers, etc. must be punished with death, whatever their creed or race.

19. We demand that the Roman Law, which serves the materialistic world order, shall be replaced by a legal system for all Germany.

20. With the aim of opening to every capable and industrious German the possibility of higher education and of thus obtaining advancement, the State must consider a thorough re-construction of our national system of education. The curriculum of all educational establishments must be brought into line with the requirements of practical life. Comprehension of the State idea (State sociology) must be the school objective, beginning with the first dawn of intelligence in the pupil. We demand development of the gifted children of poor parents, whatever their class or occupation, at the expense of the State.

21. The State must see to raising the standard of health in the nation by protecting mothers and infants, prohibiting child labour, increasing bodily efficiency by obligatory gymnastics and sports laid down by law, and by extensive support of clubs engaged in the bodily development of the young.

22. We demand abolition of a paid army and formation of a national army.

23. We demand legal warfare against conscious political lying and its dissemination in the Press. In order to facilitate creation of a German national Press we demand:

(a) that all editors of newspapers and their assistants, employing the German language, must be members of the nation;

(b) that special permission from the State shall be necessary before non-

German newspapers may appear. These are not necessarily printed in the German language;

(c) that non-Germans shall be prohibited by law from participating financially in or influencing German newspapers, and that the penalty for contravention of the law shall be suppression of any such newspaper, and immediate deportation of the non-German concerned in it.

It must be forbidden to publish papers which do not conduce to the national welfare. We demand legal prosecution of all tendencies in art and literature of a kind likely to disintegrate our life as a nation, and the suppression of institutions which militate against the requirements above-mentioned.

24. We demand liberty for all religious denominations in the State, so far as they are not a danger to it and do not militate against the moral feelings of the German race.

The Party, as such, stands for positive Christianity, but does not bind itself in the matter of creed to any particular confession. It combats the Jewish-materialist spirit within us and without us, and is convinced that our nation can only achieve permanent health from within on the principle:

THE COMMON INTEREST BEFORE SELF

25. That all the foregoing may be realised we demand the creation of a strong central power of the State. Unquestioned authority of the politically centralised Parliament over the entire Reich and its organisation; and formation of Chambers for classes and occupations for the purpose of carrying out the general laws promulgated by the Reich in the various States of the confederation.

The leaders of the Party swear to go straight forward — if necessary to sacrifice their lives — in securing fulfillment of the foregoing Points.

Munich, February 24th, 1920.

Source: Official English translation by E. Dugdale, reprinted from Kurt G. W. Ludecke, *I Knew Hitler* (New York: Charles Scribner's Sons, 1937).

APPENDIX B

Affidavit of Hjalmar Schacht

I, Dr. Hjalmar Schacht, after having been warned that I will be liable to punishment for making false statements, state herewith under oath, of my own free will and without coercion, the following:

The amounts contributed by the participants in the meeting of 20 February 1933 at Goering's house were paid by them to the bankers. Delbrück, Schickler & Co., Berlin, to the credit of an account "Nationale Treuhand" (which may be translated as National Trusteeship). It was arranged that I was entitled to dispose of this account, which I administered as a trustee, and that in case of my death, or that in case the trusteeship should be terminated in any other way, Rudolf Hess should be entitled to dispose of the account.

I disposed of the amounts of this account by writing out checks to Mr. Hess. I do not know what Mr. Hess actually did with the money.

On 4 April 1933, I closed the account with Delbrück, Schickler & Co. and had the balance transferred to the "Account Ic" with the Reichsbank which read in my name. Later on I was ordered directly by Hitler, who was authorized by the assembly of 20 February 1933 to dispose of the amounts collected, or through Hess, his deputy, to pay the balance of about 600,000 marks to Ribbentrop.

I have carefully read this affidavit (one page) and have signed it. I have made the necessary corrections in my own handwriting and initialed each correction in the margin of the page. I declare herewith under oath that I have stated the full truth to the best of my knowledge and belief.

(Signed) Dr. Hjalmar Schacht

12 August 1947

In a subsequent affidavit of 18 August 1947 (N1-9764, Pros. Ex 54), Schacht declared the following with regard to the above interrogation: "I made all of the statements appearing in this interrogation to Clifford Hyanning, a financial investigator of the American Forces of my own free will and without coercion. I have reread this interrogation today and can state that all of the facts contained therein are true to my best knowledge and belief. I declare herewith under oath and I have stated the full truth to the best of my knowledge and belief."

Source: Copy of Document Prosecution Exhibit 55. *Trials of War Criminals before the Nuremburg Military Tribunals under Control Council Law No. 10*, Nuremburg, October 1946-April 1949, Volume VII, I.G. Farben, (Washington: U.S. Government Printing Office, 1952).

APPENDIX C

Entries in the "National Trusteeship" Account Found in the Files of the Delbrück, Schickler Co. Bank

NATIONAL TRUSTEESHIP
REICHSBANK PRESIDENT DR. HJALMAR SCHACHT, BERLIN-ZEHLENDORF

Date	Description	Amount	Date	Amount
Feb. 23	Debibk (Deutsche Bank Diskonto-Gesellschaft) Verein fuer die bergbaulichen Interessen, Essen		Feb. 23	200,000.00
24	Transfer to account Rudolf Hess, at present in Berlin	100,000.00	24	
24	Karl Herrmann		25	150,000.00
	Automobile Exhibition, Berlin		25	100,000.00
25	Director A. Steinke		27	200,000.00
25	Demag A.G., Duisberg		27	50,000.00
27	Telefunken Gesellschaft fuer draht lose Telegraphie Berlin		28	35,000.00
	Osram G.m.b.H., Berlin		28	40,000.00
27	Bayerische Hypotheken- und Wechselbank, branch office Munich, Kauflingerstr. in favor of Verlag Franz Eher Nachf, Munich	100,000.00	28	
27	Transfer to account Rudolf Hess, Berlin	100,000.00	27	
28	I.G. Farbenindustrie A.G. Frankfurt/M		Mar. 1	400,000.00
28	Telegraph expenses for transfer to Munich	8.00	Feb. 28	
Mar. 1	Your Payment		Mar. 2	125,000.00

2	Telegr. transfer to Bayerische Hypotheken-und Wechselbank, Munich branch office, Bayerstr. for account Josef Jung	400,000.00	2		
	Telegr. transfer expenses	23.00	2		
	Account transfer Rudolf Hess	300,000.00			
2	Reimbursement from Director Karl Lange, Berlin		3	30,000.00
3	Reimbursement from Dir. Karl Lange, 'Maschinen-industrie' Account		4	20,000.00
	Reimbursement from Verein fuer die bergbaulichen Interessen, Essen		4	100,000.00
	Reimbursement from Karl Herrmann, Berlin, Dessauerstr. 28/9		4	150,000.00
	Reimbursement from Allgemeine Elektrizitaetsgesellschaft, Berlin		4	60,000.00
7	Reimbursement from General-direktor Dr. F. Springorum, Dortmund		8	36,000.00
8	Reichsbank transfer: Bayerische Hypotheken-und Wechselbank, branch office Kauffingerstr.	100,000.00	8	
		1,100,031.00		1,696,000.00
		1,100,031.00	Mar.	1,696,000.00

Mar.	8	Bayerische Hypotheken-und Wechselbank, Munich, branch office Bayerstr.	100,000.00	8	
		Transfer to account Rudolf Hess	250,000.00	7	
	10	Accumulatoren-Fabrik A.G. Berlin		11	25,000.00
	13	Verein f.d. bergbaulichen Interessen, Essen		14	300,000.00
	14	Reimbursement Rudolf Hess	200,000.00	14	
	29	Reimbursement Rudolf Hess	200,000.00	29	

Apr.	4	Commerz-und Privatbank Dep. Kasse N. Berlin W.9 Potsdamerstr. 1 f. Special Account S 29	99,000.00	Apr. 4	

5	Interests according to list 1 percent		5	404.50
	Phone bills	1.00	5	
	Postage	2.50	5	
	Balance	72,370.00	5	
	Balance carried over	2,021,404.50		2,021,404.50
			Apr. 5	72,370.00

APPENDIX D

Letter from U.S. War Department to Ethyl Corporation

December 15, 1934

Exhibit No. 144

(Handwritten) Mr. Webb sent copies for other Directors

Copy to: Mr. Alfred P. Sloan, Jr., General Motors Corp., New York City.
    Mr. Donaldson Brown, General Motors Corp., New York City.

December 15, 1934.

Mr. E. W. Webb,

  President Ethyl Gasoline Corporation, 135 E. 42nd Street, New York City.
Dear Mr. Webb: I learned through our Organic Chemicals Division today that the Ethyl Gasoline Corporation has in mind forming a German company with the I.G. to manufacture Ethyl lead in that country.

I have just had two weeks in Washington, no inconsiderable part of which was devoted to criticising the interchanging with foreign companies of chemical knowledge which might have a military value. Such giving of information by an industrial company might have the gravest repercussions on it. The Ethyl Gasoline Corporation would be no exception, in fact, would probably be singled out for special attack because of the ownership of its stock.

It should seem, on the face of it, that the quantity of Ethyl lead used for commercial purposes in Germany would be too small to go after. It has been claimed that Germany is secretly arming. Ethyl lead would doubtless be a valuable aid to military aeroplanes.

I am writing you this to say that in my opinion under no conditions should you or the Board of Directors of the Ethyl Gasoline Corporation disclose any secrets or 'know how' in connection with the manufacture of tetraethyl lead to Germany.

I am informed that you will be advised through the Dyestuffs Division of the necessity of disclosing the information which you have received from Germany to appropriate War Department officials.

Yours very truly,

Source: United States Senate, Hearings before a Subcommittee of the Committee on Military Affairs, *Scientific and Technical Mobilization*, 78th Congress, Second Session, Part 16, (Washington D.C.: Government Printing Office, 1944), p. 939.

APPENDIX E

Extract from Morgenthau Diary (Germany) Regarding Sosthenes Behn of I.T.T.

March 16, 1945
11:30 a.m.

GROUP MEETING
Bretton Woods — I.T.&T. — Reparations

Present:
- Mr. White
- Mr. Fussell
- Mr. Feltus
- Mr. Coe
- Mr. DuBois
- Mrs. Klotz

H.M., Jr.: Frank, can you boil down this business on I.T.&T.?

Mr. Coe: Yes, sir. I.T.&T. by the way did transfer or did get $15 million yesterday or a few days ago of their debts in dollars paid to them by the Spanish Government and that they are allowed to do under our general license, so that's all right. However, it is in part in their representation to us, part of a deal for the sale of the company in Spain, so they are trying thereby to force our hand. Now, the proposition which they have had up over some years in different forms now takes this form. They can get their receivables paid off in dollars, which they say they have not been able to do hitherto — either $15 million now and $10 million or $11 million later. They will sell the company to Spain and take in return $30 million worth of bonds — Spanish Government bonds — which are to be amortized over a number of years and roughly at the rate of $2 million per annum, and they are to receive 20% of those exports in order to amortize bonds faster, if they are to export it to the United States.

H. M. Jr.: Like the match dealer I mentioned in my speech.

Mr. Coe: That's right. The Spanish Government. They are willing, they say — they are able to get from the Spanish Government assurances, that these will not be, that the shares which the Spanish Government intends to resell will not go to anybody on the black list, and so forth. In some negotiations we have had with them over the last few weeks, they have been willing to come further on that. Our hesitation on the matter relates to two things; First, that you can't trust Franco, and that if they are able — if Franco is able to sell $50 million worth of shares of this company in Spain in the next period of time, he may very well sell it to pro-German interests. It seems doubtful that he would be able to dispose of it to the Spaniards, so that is the first thing. The second thing we can't document too well, but I think it is more pronounced in my mind than in the minds of the Foreign Funds and legal people. I don't think we can really trust Behn either.

Mr. White: I'm sure you can't.

Mr. Coe: We have records here of interviews, going far back, that some of your men had with Behn — Klaus was one — in which Behn said that he had had conversations with Goering with the proposition that Goering was to hold I.T.&T.'s property in Germany, and as you recall, I.T.&T. here did try to purchase General Aniline and make it an American company thereby and that was part of the deal which Behn told State and our lawyers very frankly he had discussed. He thought it was perfectly all right protecting property: That was before we entered the war.

H. M., Jr.: I don't remember that.

Mr. Coe: The man in charge of their properties now is Westrick who you recall came over here and was mixed up with Texaco. They tried in every way to cook up deals earlier to escape. They are tied up with top German group and etc. On the other hand, Colonel Behn has been used several times as an emissary by the State Department, and I believe he is personally on very good terms with Stettinius. We have heard from State on this letter saying they have no objections. We proposed to you earlier — the letter which I sent in to you suggesting that you ask State, if in view of our safe haven objectives, they still said yes. I am confident from talking with them on the phone the last day or two, they will write back and say yes, they still think it is a good deal.

H. M., Jr.: This is the position I am in. As you gentlemen know I am over-extended now and I can't go into this thing personally, and I think that we are just going to have to throw the thing in the lap of the State Department, and if they want to clear it, all right. I just haven't got the time or the energy to fight them on that basis.

Mr. Coe: Then we ought to license it now.

Mr. White: First you ought to get a letter. I agree with the Secretary on this point of view that this fellow Behn is not to be trusted around the corner. There is something about this deal that looks suspicious and has been for the last couple of years we have been dealing with him. However, it is one thing to believe that and another thing to defend that before the pressure that will be brought in here that they are trying to deprive this company of the business deal, but I think that what we might do is get the State Department on record that in view of a safe haven project they don't think that there is any danger that any of these assets — I would cite some of them, spell the letter out. Get them down on record and even make them a little frightened and hold out or they will at least have had the record and you will have called their attention to these dangers. This fellow Behn hates our guts anyway. We have been standing between him and deals for 4 years, at least.

H. M., Jr.: Follow what White said. Something along that line. "Dear Mr. Stet-

tinius: I am bothered about these things due to the following facts, and I would like you to advise me whether we should or should not . . . ."
Mr. White: "In view of the danger that German assets may be cloaked here, the future —" and let him come back and say, "No," and we'll watch him.
Mr. Coe: We said we wanted to give Acheson something Monday.
H. M., Jr.: And if you get that ready for me by tomorrow morning, I'll sign it.
Mr. Coe: O.K.

Source: United States Senate, Subcommittee to Investigate the Administration of the Internal Security Act. Committee on the Judiciary, *Morgenthau Diary (Germany)*, Volume 1, 90th Congress, 1st Session, November 20, 1967, (Washington D.C.: U.S. Government Printing Office, 1967), p. 320 of Book 828. (Page 976 of U.S. Senate print.)

Note: "Mr. White" is Harry Dexter White. "Dr. Dubois" is Josiah E. Dubois, Jr., author of the book, *Generals in Grey Suits* (London: The Bodley Head, 1953). "H.M., Jr." is Henry Morgenthau, Jr., Secretary of the Treasury.
    This memorandum is important because it accuses Sosthenes Behn of attempting to make behind-the-scenes deals in Nazi Germany "for 4 years, at least" — *i.e.* while the rest of the U.S. was at war, Behn and his friends were still doing business as usual with Germany. This memorandum supports the evidence presented in Chapters Five and Nine concerning the influence of I.T.T. in the Himmler inner circle and adds Herman Goering to the list of I.T.T. contacts.

FOOTNOTES

INTRODUCTION

1. (New York: Arlington House Publishers, 1974)

2. (New York: Arlington House Publishers, 1975)

3. *The Higher Circles: The Governing Class in America*, (New York: Vintage, 1970)

4. *None Dare Call It Conspiracy*, (Rossmoor: Concord Press, 1971). For another view based on "inside" documents, see Carroll Quigley, *Tragedy and Hope*, (New York: The Macmillan Company, 1966)

5. *The Invisible Government*, (Boston: Western Islands, 1962)

6. Published in English as *The Occult and the Third Reich*, (The mystical origins of Naziism and the search for the Holy Grail), (New York: The Macmillan Company, 1974). See also Reginald H. Phelps, " 'Before Hitler Came:' Thule Society and Germanen Orden" in the *Journal of Modern History*, September 1963, No. 3.

7. (Boston: Little Brown and Company, 1950)

8. Edgar B. Nixon, ed., *Franklin D. Roosevelt and Foreign Affairs*, Volume III: September 1935-January 1937, (Cambridge: Belknap Press, 1969), p. 456.

9. Edited by William E. Dodd Jr. and Martha Dodd, *Ambassador Dodd's Diary, 1933-1938*, (New York: Harcourt Brace and Company, 1941), p. 303.

10. Ibid, p. 358.

11. Quigley, *op. cit.*

12. For more information about "Putzi" Hanfstaengl, see Chapter Nine.

13. See Sutton, *Wall Street and the Bolshevik Revolution, op. cit.*, for Schacht's relations with Soviets and Wall Street, and his directorship of a Soviet bank.

CHAPTER ONE

1. United States Congress. Senate. Hearings before a Subcommittee of the Committee on Military Affairs. *Elimination of German Resources for War.* Report pursuant to S. Res. 107 and 146, July 2, 1945, Part 7, (78th Congress and 79th Congress), (Washington: Government Printing Office, 1945), hereafter cited as *Elimination of German Resources.*

2. *Elimination of German Resources*, p. 174.

3. Gabriel Kolko, "American Business and Germany, 1930-1941," *The Western Political Quarterly*, Volume XV, 1962.

4. Ibid, p. 715.

5. Carroll Quigley, *op. cit.*

6. Ibid, p. 308.

7. Carroll Quigley, *op. cit.*, p. 309.

8. Fritz Thyssen, *I Paid Hitler*, (New York: Farrar & Rinehart, Inc., n.d.), p. 88.

9. U.S. Group Control Council (Germany), Office of the Director of Intelligence, Intelligence Report No. EF/ME/1, 4 September 1945. Also see Hjalmar Schacht, *Confessions of "the old Wizard"*, (Boston: Houghton Mifflin, 1956)

10. Hjalmar Schacht, *op. cit.*, p. 18. Fritz Thyssen adds, "Even at the time Mr. Dillon, a New York Banker of Jewish origin whom I much admire told me 'In your place I would not sign the plan.'"

11. Ibid, p. 232.

12. Carroll Quigley, *op. cit.*, p. 324.

13. Henry H. Schloss, *The Bank for International Settlements* (Amsterdam: North Holland Publishing Company, 1958)

14. John Hargrave, *Montagu Norman*, (New York: The Greystone Press, n.d.), p. 108.

15. James Stewart Martin, *op. cit.*, p. 70.

16. See Chapter Seven for more details of Wall Street loans to German industry.

17. See Gabriel Kolko, *op. cit.*, for numerous examples.

18. In 1956 the Chase and Manhattan banks merged to become Chase Manhattan.

CHAPTER TWO

1. German firms have a two-tier board of directors. The *Aufsichsrat* concerns itself with overall supervision, including financial policy, while the *Vorstand* is concerned with day-to-day management.

2. Taken from *Der Farben-Konzern 1928*, (Hoppenstedt, Berlin: 1928), pp. 4-5.

3. *Elimination of German Resources*, p. 943.

4. Ibid, p. 945.

5. *New York Times*, October 21, 1945, Section 1, pp. 1, 12.

6. Ibid, p. 947.

7. *Elimination of German Resources*.

8 Bernhard is today better known for his role as chairman of the secretive, so-called Bilderberger meetings. See U.S. Congress, House of Representatives, Special Committee on Un-American Activities, *Investigation of Nazi Propaganda Activities and Investigation of Certain other Propaganda Activities.* 73rd Congress, 2nd Session, Hearings No. 73-DC-4. (Washington: Government Printing Office, 1934), Volume VIII, p. 7323.

9. Ibid, p. 949.

10. Ibid, p. 952.

11. Ibid, p. 1293.

12. Ibid, p. 954.

13. Ibid, p. 954.

14. Ibid, pp. 954-5.

15. U.S. Congress. House of Representatives, Special Committee on Un-American Activities, *Investigation of Nazi Propaganda Activities and Investigation of Certain Other Propaganda Activities, op. cit.*

16. Ibid, p. 178.

17. Ibid, p. 183.

18. Ibid, p. 188.

CHAPTER THREE

1. For the technical details see the three-volume study, Antony C. Sutton, *Western Technology and Soviet Economic Development,* (Stanford, California: Hoover Institution Press, 1968, 1971, 1973), hereafter cited as *Western Technology Series.*

2. (New York: Arlington House Publishers, 1975)

3. *New York Times,* October 6, 1936. See also Antony C. Sutton, *Wall Street and FDR, op. cit.*

4. Of course, socialist pleading by businessmen is still with us. Witness the injured cries when President Ford proposed deregulation of airlines and trucking. See for example *Wall Street Journal,* November 25, 1975.

5. Mimeographed Translation in Hoover Institution Library, p. 67. Also see Walter Rathenau, *In Days to Come,* (London: Allen & Unwin, n.d.)

6. Ibid, p. 249.

7. *New York Times,* July 2, 1929.

8. Ibid, July 28, 1929.

9. Ibid, August 2, 1929 and August 4, 1929.

10. Ibid, August 6, 1929.

11. Ibid, February 2, 1930.

12. Ibid, February 2, 1930.

13. Ibid, May 11, 1930. For the prewar machinations of General Electric, Osram, and the Dutch company N.V. Philips Gloeilampenfabrieken of Eindhoven Holland, see Chapter 11, "Electric Eels," in James Stewart Martin, *op cit.* Martin was Chief of the Economic Warfare Division of the U.S. Department of Justice and comments that "The A.E.G. of Germany was largely controlled by the American company, General Electric." The assumption by this author is that the G.E. influence was somewhat less than controlling although substantial enough. Because of Martin's official position and access to official documents, not known to the author, his statement that A.E.G. was "largely controlled" by U.S. General Electric cannot be lightly dismissed. However, if we accept that G.E. "largely controlled" A.E.G., then the most serious questions arise which clamor for investigation. A.E.G. was a prime financier of Hitler and "control" would more deeply implicate the U.S. parent company than is suggested by the evidence presented here.

14. Son of Emil Rathenau, founder of A.E.G., born in 1867 and assassinated in 1922.

15. The United States Strategic Bombing Survey, *German Electrical Equipment Industry Report*, (Equipment Division, January 1947), p. 4.

16. U.S. Strategic Bombing Survey, *Plant Report of A.E.G. (Allgemeine Elektrizitats Gesellschaft)*, Nuremburg, Germany: June 1945), p. 6.

17. p. 3. Consequently, "production during the war was adequate until November 1944" and "in the opinion of Speer assistants and plant officials the war effort in Germany was never hindered in any important manner by any shortage of electrical equipment." Difficulties arose only at the very end of the war when the whole economy was threatened with collapse. The report concluded, "All important needs for electrical equipment in 1944 may therefore be said to have been met, since plans were always optimistic."

18. U.S. Strategic Bombing Survey, *AEG-Ostlandwerke GmbH*, by Whitworth Ferguson, 31 May 1945.

CHAPTER FOUR

1. In 1935, John D. Rockefeller, Jr. owned stock valued at $245 million in Standard Oil of New Jersey, Standard Oil of California, and Socony-Vacuum Company, *New York Times*, January 10, 1935.

2. *Elimination of German Resources, op cit.*, p. 1085.

3. Ibid.

4. *NMT*, I.G. Farben case, p. 1304.

5. *New York Times*, April 28, 1929.

6. Ibid.

7. Ibid, November 24, 1929.

8. *NMT*, I.G. Farben case, Volumes VII and VIII, pp. 1304-1311.

9. See letter from U.S. War Department reproduced as Appendix D.

10. United States Congress. Senate. Hearings before a subcommittee of the Committee on Military Affairs. *Scientific and Technical Mobilization*, (78th Congress, 1st session, S. 702), Part 16, (Washington: Government Printing Office, 1944), p. 939. Hereafter cited as *Scientific and Technical Mobilization*.

11. Ibid.

12. *Oil and Petroleum Yearbook, 1938*, p. 89.

13. *New York Times*, October 19, 1945, p. 9.

14. George W. Stocking & Myron W. Watkins, *Cartels in Action*, (New York: The Twentieth Century Fund, 1946), p. 9.

15. For original documents see *NMT*, I.G. Farben case, Volume VIII, pp. 1189-94.

16. *NMT*, I.G. Farben case, Volume VIII, p. 1264-5.

17. *Scientific and Technical Mobilization*, p. 543.

18. Robert Engler, *The Politics of Oil*, (New York: The MacMillan Company, 1961), p. 102.

19. See Chapter Nine for details.

CHAPTER FIVE

1. For an excellent review of I.T.T.'s worldwide activities, see Anthony Sampson, *The Sovereign State of I.T.T.*, (New York: Stein & Day, 1973).

2. See also Sutton, *Wall Street and the Bolshevik Revolution, op. cit.*

3. *New York Times*, August 4, 1933.

4. See also Chapter Nine for documentary proof of these I.T.T. payments to the S.S.

5. *Elimination of German Resources*, p. 871.

6. Ibid.

7. *New York Times*, July 20, 1936.

8. Anthony Sampson reports a meeting between I.T.T. vice president Kenneth Stockton and Westrick in which the preservation of I.T.T. properties was planned. See Anthony Sampson, *op. cit.*, p. 39.

9. There is no substance to reports that Rieber received $20,000 from the Nazis. These reports were investigated by the F.B.I. with no proof forthcoming. See

United States Senate, Subcommittee to Investigate the Administration of the Internal Security Act, Committee on the Judiciary, *Morgenthau Diary (Germany)*, Volume I, 90th Congress, 1st Session, November 20, 1967, (Washington: U.S. Government Printing Office, 1967), pp. 316-8. On Rieber see also *Appendix to the Congressional Record*, August 20, 1942, p. A 1301-2, Remarks of Hon. John M. Coffee.

10. See pp. 128-130 for further details.

11. James Stewart Martin, *op. cit.*, p. 52.

CHAPTER SIX

1. June 4, 1938, 2:2.

2. A list of these Gorki vehicles and their model numbers is in Antony C. Sutton, *National Suicide: Military Aid to the Soviet Union*, (New York: Arlington House Publishers, 1973), Table 7-2, p. 125.

3. The House of Morgan was known for its anti-Semitic views.

4. Page 2, Column 3.

5. Ibid.

6. Jonathan Leonard, *The Tragedy of Henry Ford*, (New York: G.P. Putnam's Sons, 1932), p. 208. Also see U.S. State Department Decimal File, National Archives Microcopy M 336, Roll 30, Document 862.00S/6, "Money sources of Hitler," a report from the U.S. Embassy in Berlin.

7. On this see Keith Sward, *The Legend of Henry Ford*, (New York: Rinehart & Co, 1948), p. 139.

8. *New York Times*, August 1, 1938.

9. Ibid., December 1, 1938, 12:2.

10. Ibid., December 19, 1938, 5:3.

11. *Elimination of German Resources*, p. 656.

12. *Elimination of German Resources*, pp. 657-8.

13. Josiah E. Dubois, Jr., *Generals in Grey Suits*, (London: The Bodley Head, 1953), p. 248.

14. Ibid., p. 249.

15. Ibid., p. 251.

16. Ibid.

17. U.S. Army Air Force, *Aiming point report No 1.E.2*, May 29, 1943.

18. U.S. State Department Decimal File, 800/61o.1.

19. Ibid.

CHAPTER SEVEN

1. *The American Historical Review*, Volume LC, No. 4, July, 1955, p. 830.

2. Ibid, fn. (2).

3. *Elimination of German Resources*, p. 648. The Albert Voegler mentioned in the Kilgore Committee list of early Hitler supporters was the German representative on the Dawes Plan Commission. Owen Young of General Electric (see Chapter Three) was a U.S. representative for the Dawes Plan and formulated its successor, the Young Plan.

4. Antony C. Sutton, *Wall Street and the Bolshevik Revolution, op. cit.*

5. *Preussiche Zeitung*, January 3, 1937.

6. See p. 116.

7. Glyn Roberts, *The Most Powerful Man in the World*, (New York: Covici, Friede, 1938), p. 305.

8. Ibid., p. 313.

9. Ibid., p. 322.

10. See *Chambre des Députés — Debats*, February 11, 1932, pp. 496-500.

11. U.S. Group Control Council (Germany, Office of the Director of Intelligence, Field Information Agency, Technical). Intelligence Report No. EF/ME/1, 4 September 1945. "Examination of Dr. Fritz Thyssen," p. 13. Hereafter cited as Examination of Dr. Fritz Thyssen.

12. The Bank was known in Germany as *Bank für Handel und Schiff*.

13. Examination of Dr. Fritz Thyssen.

14. Fritz Thyssen, *I Paid Hitler*, (New York: Farrar & Rinehart, Inc., 1941), p. 159.

15. Taken from *Bankers Directory*, 1932 edition, p. 2557 and Poors, *Directory of Directors*. J.L. Guinter and Knight Woolley were also directors.

16. See Antony C. Sutton, *Wall Street and the Bolshevik Revolution, op. cit.*

17. *National Cyclopaedia*, Volume G, page 16.

18. For a description of these ventures, based on State Department files, see Antony C. Sutton, *Western Technology and Soviet Economic Development*, Volume 1, *op. cit.*

19. See Antony C. Sutton, *Wall Street and FDR*, Chapter Nine, "Swope's Plan," *op. cit.*

20. See *Elimination of German Resources*, pp. 728-30.

21. For yet other connections between the Union Banking Corp. and German enterprises, see Ibid., pp. 728-30.

22. See Chapter Ten.

23. *NMT*, Volume VII, p. 555.

24. Josiah E. Dubois, Jr., *Generals in Grey Suits op. cit.*, p. 323.

25. Original reproduced on page 64.

26. *NMT*, Volume VII, p. 565. See p. 64 for photograph of original document.

27. Fritz Thyssen, *I Paid Hitler*, (New York: Toronto: Farrar & Rinehart, Inc., 1941).

28. *NMT*, Volume VI, pp. 1169-1170.

29. *NMT*, Volume VII, p. 565.

CHAPTER EIGHT

1. William E. Dodd, *Ambassador Dodd's Diary, 1933-1938*, (New York: Harcourt, Brace & Co., 1941), p. 360.

2. Ernst Hanfstaengl, *Unheard Witness*, (New York: J.B. Lippincott, 1957), p. 28.

3. Ibid., p.

4. Ibid., p. 52.

5. Ibid., p. 53.

6. Ibid., p. 59.

7. Ibid., p. 122.

8. Ibid., pp. 197-8.

9. Ibid., p. 214.

10. Ladislas Farago, *The Game of the Foxes*, (New York: Bantam, 1973), p. 97.

11. Ibid., p. 106.

12. Ernst Hanfstaengl, *Unheard Witness, op. cit.*, p. 76.

13. Ibid.

14. Ibid., pp. 310-11.

15. *Dustbin* report EF/Me/1. Interview of Thyssen, p. 13.

16. Hjalmar Horace Greeley Schacht, *Confessions of "The Old Wizard,"* (Boston: Houghton Mifflin, 1956), p. 276.

17. George Dimitrov, *The Reichstag Fire Trial*, (London: The Bodley Head, 1934), p. 309.

18. Ibid., p. 310.

19. Ibid., p. 311.

20. Helmut Magers, *Ein Revolutionar Aus Common Sense*, (Leipzig: R. Kittler Verlag, 1934).

21. Nixon, Edgar B., Editor, *Franklin D. Roosevelt and Foreign Affairs*, (Cambridge: The Belknap Press of Harvard University Press, 1969), Volume 1: January 1933-February 1934. Franklin D. Roosevelt Library. Hyde Park, New York.

CHAPTER NINE

1. From the affidavit of Wilhem Keppler, *NMT*, Volume VI, p. 285.

2. *Elimination of German Resources*, p. 869.

3. *NMT*, Volume VII, p. 238. "Translation of Document N1-10103, Prosecution Exhibit 788." Letter from von Schröder and Defendant Steinbrinck to Dr. Meyer, Dresdner Bank official, 25 February 1936, noting that the Circle of Friends would put funds at Himmler's disposal "For Certain Tasks outside of the Budget" and had established a "Special Account for this purpose."

4. *Elimination of German Resources*, p. 857.

5. The significant nature of this representation is reflected in Chart 8-1, "Wall Street representation in the Keppler and Himmler Circles, 1933 and 1944."

CHAPTER TEN

1. William E. Dodd, *Ambassador Dodd's Diary, op. cit.*, p. 31.

2. Ibid., p. 74.

3. Franz von Papen, *Memoirs*, (New York: E.P. Dutton & Co., 1953), p. 229.

4. The English text for this chapter is translated from an authenticated surviving German translation of a copy of the Dutch edition of *De Geldbronnen van Het Nationaal-Socialisme (Drie Gesprekken Met Hitler)*, or *The Financial Sources of National Socialism (Three conversations with Hitler.* The original Dutch author is given as "Door Sidney Warburg, vertaald door I.G. Shoup" (By Sidney Warburg, as told by I.G. Shoup).

   The copy used here was translated from the Dutch by Dr. Walter Nelz, Wilhelm Peter, and Rene Sonderegger in Zurich, February 11, 1947, and the German translation bears an affidavit to the effect that: "The undersigned three witnesses do verify that the accompanying document is none other than a true and literal translation from Dutch into German of the book by Sidney Warburg, a copy of which was constantly at their disposal during the complete process of translation. They testify that they held this original in their hands, and that to the best of their ability they read it sentence by sentence, translating it into German, comparing then the content of the accompanying translation to the original conscientiously until complete agreement was reached."

5. Note that "von Heydt" was the original name for the Dutch Bank voor

Handel en Scheepvaart N.V., a subsidiary of the Thyssen interests and now known to have been used as a funnel for Nazi funds. See *Elimination of German Resources.*

6. Examination of the index for the *New York Times* confirms the accuracy of the latter part of this statement. See for example the sudden rush of interest by the *New York Times,* September 15, 1930 and the feature article on "Hitler, Driving Force in Germany's Fascism" in the September 21, 1930 issue of the *New York Times.* In 1929 the *New York Times* listed only one brief item on Adolf Hitler. In 1931 it ran a score of substantial entries, including no fewer than three "Portraits."

7. Hoover said he lost the support of Wall Street in 1931 because he would not go along with its plan for a New Deal: see Antony C. Sutton, *Wall Street and FDR, op. cit.*

8. Franz von Papen, *Memoirs,* (New York: E.P. Dutton & Co., Inc., 1953). Translated by Brian Connell.

9. Werner Zimmerman, *Liebet Eure Feinde,* (Frankhauser Verlag: Thielle-Neuchatel, 1948), which contains a chapter, "Hitler's geheime Geldgeber" (Hitler's secret financial supporters) and Rene Sonderegger, *Spanischer Sommer,* (Affoltern, Switzerland: Aehren Verlag, 1948).

10. Franz von Papen, *Memoirs, op. cit.,* p. 23.

11. William E. Dodd, *Ambassador Dodd's Diary, op. cit.* pp. 593-602.

12. The reader should examine the complete Warburg statement and affidavit; see Franz von Papen, *Memoirs, op. cit.* pp. 593-602.

13. Franz von Papen, *Memoirs, op. cit.,* p. 594.

14. See Antony C. Sutton, *Wall Street and the Bolshevik Revolution, op. cit.*

CHAPTER ELEVEN

1. *Morgenthau Diary (Germany).*

2. Ibid.

3. Ibid.

4. Ibid., pp. 800-2.

5. James Stewart Martin, *All Honorable Men, op. cit.,* p. 75.

6. *Morgenthau Diary (Germany),* p. 1543. Colonel Graeme K. Howard's book was entitled, *America and a New World Order,* (New York: Scribners, 1940).

7. The reader should examine the essay, "The Return to War Crimes," in James J. Martin, *Revisionist Viewpoints,* (Colorado: Ralph Mules, 1971).

8. *Elimination of German Resources,* p. 652.

CHAPTER TWELVE

1. Carroll Quigley, *Tragedy and Hope, op. cit.*

2. There are many others; the author selected more or less at random two conservatives (Allen and Lasell) and two liberals (Archer and Domhoff).

3. Percy L. Greaves, Jr., "The Pearl Harbor Investigation," in Harry Elmer Harnes, *Perpetual War for Perpetual Peace*, (Caldwell: Caxton Printers, 1953), p. 13-20.

4. Colin Simpson, *Lusitania*, (London: Longman, 1972), p. 252.

5. Jules Archer, *The Plot to Seize the White House*, (New York: Hawthorn Book, 1973), p. 202.

6. See Julius Epstein, *Operation Keelhaul*, (Old Greenwich: Devin Adair, 1973).

7. See for example Robert Welch, *The Politician*, (Belmont, Mass.: Belmont Publishing Co., 1963).

SELECTED BIBLIOGRAPHY

Allen, Gary. *None Dare Call It Conspiracy*. Seal Beach, California: Concord Press, 1971.

Ambruster, Howard Watson. *Treason's Peace*. New York: The Beechhurst Press, 1947.

Angebert, Michel. *The Occult and the Third Reich*. New York: The Macmillan Company, 1974.

Archer, Jules. *The Plot to Seize the White House*. New York: Hawthorn Books, 1973.

Baker, Philip Noel. *Hawkers of Death*. The Labour Party, England, 1934.

Barnes, Harry Elmer. *Perpetual War for Perpetual Peace*. Caldwell, Idaho: Caxton Printers, 1953.

Bennett, Edward W. *Germany and the Diplomacy of the Financial Crisis, 1931*. Cambridge: Harvard University Press, 1962.

Der Farben-Konzern 1928. Hoppenstedt, Berlin, 1928.

Dimitrov, George, *The Reichstag Fire Trial*. London: The Bodley Head, 1934.

Dodd, William E. Jr., and Dodd, Martha. *Ambassador Dodd's Diary, 1933-1938*. New York: Harcourt Brace and Company, 1941.

Domhoff, G. William. *The Higher Circles: The Governing Class in America*. New York: Vintage, 1970.

Dubois, Josiah E., Jr. *Generals in Grey Suits*. London: The Bodley Head, 1953.

Engelbrecht, H.C. *Merchants of Death*. New York: Dodd, Mead & Company, 1934.

Engler, Robert. *The Politics of Oil*. New York: The Macmillan Company, 1961.

Epstein, Julius. *Operation Keelhaul*. Old Greenwich: Devin Adair, 1973.

Farago, Ladislas. *The Game of the Foxes*. New York: Bantam, 1973.

Flynn, John T. *As We Go Marching*. New York: Doubleday, Doran and Co., Inc., 1944.

Guerin, Daniel. *Fascisme et grand capital*. Paris: Francois Maspero, 1965.

Hanfstaengl, Ernst. *Unheard Witness*. New York: J. B. Lippincott, 1957.

Hargrave, John. *Montagu Norman*. New York: The Greystone Press, n.d..

Harris, C.R.S. *Germany's Foreign Indebtedness*. London: Oxford University Press, 1935.

Helfferich, Dr. Karl. *Germany's Economic Progress and National Wealth, 1888-1913*. New York: Germanistic Society of America, 1914.

Hexner, Ervin. *International Cartels*. Chapel Hill: The University of North Carolina Press, 1945.

Howard, Colonel Graeme K. *America and a New World Order*. New York: Scribners, 1940.

Kolko, Gabriel. "American Business and Germany, 1930-1941," *The Western Political Quarterly*, Volume XV, 1962.

Kuczynski, Robert R. *Bankers' Profits from German Loans*. Washington, D.C.: The Brookings Institution, 1932.

Leonard, Jonathan. *The Tragedy of Henry Ford*. New York: G.P. Putnam's Sons, 1932.

Ludecke, Kurt G.W. *I Knew Hitler*. New York: Charles Scribner's Sons, 1937.

Magers, Helmut. *Ein Revolutionar Aus Common Sense*. Leipzig: R. Kittler Verlag, 1934.

Martin, James J. *Revisionist Viewpoints*. Colorado: Ralph Mules, 1971.

Martin, James Stewart. *All Honorable Men*. Boston: Little Brown and Company, 1950.

Muhlen, Norbert. *Schacht: Hitler's Magician*. New York: Longmans, Green and Co., 1939.

Nixon, Edgar B. *Franklin D. Roosevelt and Foreign Affairs*. Cambridge: Belknap Press, 1969.

Oil and Petroleum Yearbook, 1938.

Papen, Franz von. *Memoirs*. New York: E.P. Dutton & Co., 1953.

Peterson, Edward Norman. *Hjalmar Schacht*. Boston: The Christopher Publishing House, 1954.

Phelps, Reginald H. *"Before Hitler Came": Thule Society and Germanen Orden*, in the *Journal of Modern History*, September, 1963.

Quigley, Carroll, *Tragedy and Hope*. New York: The Macmillan Company, 1966.

Ravenscroft, Trevor. *The Spear of Destiny*. New York: G.P. Putnam's Sons, 1973.

Rathenau, Walter. *In Days to Come*. London: Allen & Unwin, n.d.

Roberts, Glyn. *The Most Powerful Man in the World*. New York: Covici, Friede, 1938.

Sampson, Anthony. *The Sovereign State of I.T.T.* New York: Stein & Day, 1973.

Schacht, Hjalmar. *Confessions of "The Old Wizard."* Boxton: Houghton Mifflin, 1956.

Schloss, Henry H. *The Bank for International Settlements*. Amsterdam: North Holland Publishing Company, 1958.

Seldes, George. *Iron, Blood and Profits*. New York and London: Harper & Brothers Publishers, 1934.

Simpson, Colin. *Lusitania*. London: Longman, 1972.

Smoot, Dan. *The Invisible Government*. Boston: Western Islands, 1962.

Strasser, Otto. *Hitler and I*. London: Jonathan Cape, n.d.

Sonderegger, Rene. *Spanischer Sommer*. Affoltern, Switzerland: Aehren Verlag, 1948.

Stocking, George W. and Watkins, Myron W. *Cartels in Action*. New York: The Twentieth Century Fund, 1946.

Sutton, Antony C. *National Suicide: Military Aid to the Soviet Union*. New York: Arlington House Publishers, 1973.

_____ *Wall Street and the Bolshevik Revolution*. New York: Arlington House Publishers, 1974.

_____ *Wall Street and FDR*. New York: Arlington House Publishers, 1975.

_____ *Western Technology and Soviet Economic Development, 1917-1930*. Stanford, California: Hoover Institution Press, 1968.

_____ *Western Technology and Soviet Economic Development, 1930-1945*. Stanford, California: Hoover Institution Press, 1971.

_____ *Western Technology and Soviet Economic Development, 1945-1965*. Stanford, California: Hoover Institution Press, 1973.

Sward, Keith. *The Legend of Henry Ford.* New York: Rinehart & Co., 1948.

Thyssen, Fritz. *I Paid Hitler.* New York: Farrar & Rinehart, Inc., n.d.

"Trials of War Criminals Before the Nuremburg Military Tribunals Under Control Council Law No. 10," Volume VIII, I.G. Farben case, Nuremburg, October 1946-April 1949. Washington: Government Printing Office, 1953.

United States Army Air Force, Aiming point report No. 1.E.2 of May 29, 1943.

United States Senate, Hearings before the Committee on Finance. *Sale of Foreign Bonds or Securities in the United States.* 72nd Congress, 1st Session, S. Res. 19, Part 1, December 18, 19, and 21, 1931. Washington: Government Printing Office, 1931.

United States Senate, Hearings before a Subcommittee of the Committee on Military Affairs. *Scientific and Technical Mobilization.* 78th Congress, 2nd Session, S. Res. 107, Part 16, August 29 and September 7, 8, 12, and 13, 1944. Washington: Government Printing Office, 1944.

United States Congress. House of Representatives. *Special Committee on Un-American Activities and Investigation of Certain Other Propaganda Activities.* 73rd Congress, 2nd Session, Hearings No. 73-DC-4. Washington: Government Printing Office, 1934.

United States Congress. House of Representatives. Special Committee on Un-American Activities (1934). *Investigation of Nazi and other Propaganda Activities.* 74th Congress, 1st Session, Report No. 153. Washington: Government Printing Office, 1934.

United States Congress. Senate. Hearings before a Subcommittee of the Committee on Military Affairs. *Elimination of German Resources for War.* Report pursuant to S. Res. 107 and 146, July 2, 1945, Part 7. 78th Congress and 79th Congress. Washington: Government Printing Office, 1945.

United States Congress. Senate. Hearings before a Subcomittee of the Committee on Military Affairs. *Scientific and Technical Mobilization.* 78th Congress, 1st session, S. 702, Part 16, Washington: Government Printing Office, 1944.

United States Group Control Council (Germany), Office of the Director of Intelligence, Field Information Agency. Technical Intelligence Report No. EF/ME/1. September 4, 1945.

United States Sente. Subcommittee to Investigate the Administration of the Internal Security Act, Committee on the Judiciary. *Morgenthau*

Diary (Germany). Volume 1, 90th Congress, 1st Session, November 20, 1967. Washington: U.S. Government Printing Office, 1967.

United States State Department Decimal File.

United States Strategic Bombing Survey. *AEG-Ostlandwerke GmbH*, by Whitworth Ferguson. 31 May 1945.

United States Strategic Bombing Survey. *German Electrical Equipment Industry Report*. Equipment Division, January 1947.

United States Strategic Bombing Survey. *Plant Report of A.E.G.* (Allgemeine Elektrizitats Gesellschaft). Nuremburg, Germany: June 1945.

Zimmerman, Werner. *Liebet Eure Feinde*. Frankhauser Verlag: Thielle-Neuchatel, 1948.

INDEX

F

G

H